The Business of Android Apps Development

Making and Marketing Apps that Succeed
on Google Play, Amazon App Store and More

Roy Sandberg
Mark Rollins

Apress®

The Business of Android Apps Development: Making and Marketing Apps that Succeed on Google Play, Amazon App Store and More

ISBN-13 (pbk): 978-1-4302-5007-4

ISBN-13 (electronic): 978-1-4302-5008-1

President and Publisher: Paul Manning
Lead Editor: Steve Anglin
Development Editor: Tom Welsh
Technical Reviewers: Bradley Brown, Gregg Petri, Harold Shinsato
Editorial Board: Steve Anglin, Mark Beckner, Ewan Buckingham, Gary Cornell, Louise Corrigan, Morgan Ertel,
  Jonathan Gennick, Jonathan Hassell, Robert Hutchinson, Michelle Lowman, James Markham,
  Matthew Moodie, Jeff Olson, Jeffrey Pepper, Douglas Pundick, Ben Renow-Clarke, Dominic Shakeshaft,
  Gwenan Spearing, Matt Wade, Tom Welsh
Coordinating Editor: Anamika Panchoo
Copy Editor: Nancy Sixsmith
Compositor: SPi Global
Indexer: SPi Global
Artist: SPi Global
Cover Designer: Anna Ishchenko

Distributed to the book trade worldwide by Springer Science+Business Media New York, 233 Spring Street, 6th Floor, New York, NY 10013. Phone 1-800-SPRINGER, fax (201) 348-4505, e-mail orders-ny@springer-sbm.com, or visit www.springeronline.com. Apress Media, LLC is a California LLC and the sole member (owner) is Springer Science + Business Media Finance Inc (SSBM Finance Inc). SSBM Finance Inc is a Delaware corporation.

For information on translations, please e-mail rights@apress.com, or visit www.apress.com.

Apress and friends of ED books may be purchased in bulk for academic, corporate, or promotional use. eBook versions and licenses are also available for most titles. For more information, reference our Special Bulk Sales–eBook Licensing web page at www.apress.com/bulk-sales.

Any source code or other supplementary materials referenced by the author in this text is available to readers at www.apress.com. For detailed information about how to locate your book's source code, go to www.apress.com/source-code/.

Contents at a Glance

Contents

About the Authors

Roy Sandberg loves the intersection of business and technology. With experience managing both engineering and operations, he has founded multiple companies. These companies' award-winning products have been sold around the world, protected by multiple issued and pending patents.

Roy trained in electrical engineering and computer science at Carnegie-Mellon University, and graduated from law school with honors. He has worked in a diverse range of technical fields, including motion control, consumer electronics, telecommunications, biotech, patent law, robotics, assistive technology, and music technology.

Roy's Android applications, released under the Sandberg Sound brand, use cutting-edge, signal-processing techniques to simplify the lives of musicians and DJs.

Roy lives in the Haight-Ashbury neighborhood of San Francisco. He always likes to hear from his readers and fellow entrepreneurs, so please don't hesitate to contact him.

Mark Rollins was born in Seattle in 1971 and attended Washington State University in Pullman, Washington, graduating in 1994 with a degree in English. After college, he began to write skits for college-age groups.

In 2005, after a career at Schweitzer Engineering Laboratories (SEL), Mark decided to pursue his dream and began writing full-time.

Mark has written for many tech and gadget blogs, including screenhead.com, image-acquire.com, cybertheater.com, mobilewhack.com, carbuyersnotebook.com, gearlive.com, zmogo.com, gadgetell.com, gadgets-weblog.com, androidedge.com, and coolest-gadgets.com. He has also written for video game blogs such as gamertell.com and digitalbattle.com.

In 2009, Mark decided to create his own tech and gadget blog known as www.TheGeekChurch.com. The purpose of the blog was to report on the latest in technology, as well as to inform the church-going crowd (who are often not very technically adept) on the benefits of using more technology in the ministry. Since 2012, Mark has completely devoted his time to helping other tech businesses succeed.

Mark currently resides in Pullman, Washington with his wife and three children.

About the Technical Reviewers

Gregg Petri has extensive experience in developing custom software applications and products, specializing in Java and Oracle Databases. He holds a BS in Applied Computer Science from Illinois State University, an MS in Computer Science from North Central College, and an MBA from the University of Denver. Gregg is currently the Director of Development in the Enterprise IT Solutions group of Rolta India, Ltd. Gregg lives in Golden, Colorado with his wife Aimee, son Chase, and twin daughters Madigan and Taryn.

 **Harold Shinsato** is a senior software engineer at SAP working with Java, Perl, C++, Bash, Jenkins, Groovy, and Ruby; and has played with Android apps on the side. He is the founder and chief facilitator of the annual unconference, Missoula Barcamp. Harold is an Open Space facilitator and board member of the Open Space Institute, professional life and agile coach, private pilot, drummer, MIT grad, and alumnus of Xerox PARC as part of the Inxight spin-out. He lives in Montana with seven sheep, a llama, two cats, and his beloved wife, Wind, who occasionally blogs at http://shinsato.com.

Acknowledgments

Roy's dad instilled in him a love of technology, and Roy's mom cultivated his love of books. It is only fitting for him to dedicate this, his first book, to his parents, Robert and Dalia Sandberg.

Roy would also like to thank the editors and staff at Apress for all their help and insight.

Finally, Roy thanks Mark Rollins for extending him this opportunity, for his hard work, and for his patient understanding when Roy made annoying last minute changes to the manuscript.

—Roy Sandberg

I would like to dedicate this book to Michelle Lowman, Steve Anglin, and Anamika Panchoo, the editors of this book. I believe that Steve was instrumental in getting me my first book deal, which was the first edition of this book.

I would also like to thank the technical editors for their efforts. I am certain that they worked hard.

I also want to thank Brian Dorgan, a very bright programmer without whom I could have never written the first edition of the book.

I also want to thank Roy. He was a joy to work with, and was very good at doing the parts that I had a hard time doing.

—Mark Rollins

Introduction

Hi, it's Mark and … I'm back! Some of you might remember the first edition of this work. I focused on the very early part of the learning curve for new Android app developers—such as what to do even if you have never heard of the Android operating system or marketplace. I demonstrated how to download programs such as Java and the Eclipse IDE, and showed you a thing or two about programming using these software tools. I also introduced subjects that are basic to marketing anything, such as reaching a target audience, establishing your application's "culture," spreading the word about your applications through various online and print sources, how to publish on Google Play (then called Android Market), and what to do after your initial launch. For the most part, I believe that I succeeded in my endeavor, but even more is required if you really want to establish yourself in the midst of a crowded Android market.

For this second edition of the book, I teamed up with Roy Sandberg, an experienced Android app developer. Roy talks about his experiences developing and marketing apps under his Sandberg Sound label (www.sandbergsound.com). Roy also does contracting work for Android, so you might want to contact him if you need a level of support that exceeds what this and other books can provide. You can find his e-mail address on his website, www.sandbergsound.com. Roy also has a background in communications theory, robotics, audio, and digital signal processing. Believe me when I say that hairy technical problems make him happy! Roy knows the technical, business, and, in some cases, legal issues encompassing the Android development process. He created a family of apps that use clever sound-processing algorithms to do some interesting things. More importantly, you'll learn from his "boots on the ground" experiences with marketing his apps. He'll let you know what worked for him and, perhaps more importantly, what didn't work.

As the author of the first edition of *The Business of Android Apps Development*, I am quite glad to have Roy on board. As for this second edition, it is not really a sequel, but more of a redux. Just so I can set your mind on the right track, this isn't really a book on how to create that million-dollar idea for an app or how to write all the code for that million-dollar app. Of course, creating and programming that application is a necessary part of Android marketing, and we'll give you some guidance in that area, but building the application is only one essential step to creating an application that will shine in the very crowded world of Android applications.

This book focuses on how to navigate marketing in the world of Android, and what it takes to make an Android app really shine. From the moment you first conceive of an app idea, all the way to supporting an existing application, we'll explain the best way to get things done.

The Purpose of this Book

It might be easier to explain what this book isn't instead of going into detail about what it is. This is not, at its heart, a programming book. Although we will give you a quick overview of programming on Android, you will have to look elsewhere for all the details. Rather, this book gives a high-level overview of all the considerations a developer must balance when bringing a new Android application to market.

As far as programming goes, we will certainly point you in the right direction, so if you're a beginning programmer, this book is a great way to get oriented. We suggest you also check out some other books from Apress:

- *Android Apps for Absolute Beginners,* by Wallace Jackson

- *Beginning Android 3,* by Mark Murphy

- *Pro Android,* by Satya Komatineni, Sayed Hashimi, and Dave MacLean

- *Pro Android 2,* by Satya Komatineni, Sayed Hashimi, and Dave MacLean

- *Pro Android 3,* by Satya Komatineni, Sayed Hashimi, and Dave MacLean

- *Pro Android Web Apps,* by Damon Oehlman and Sébastien Blanc

- *Android Essentials,* by Chris Haseman

- *Learn Java for Android Development,* by Jeff Friesen

It is essential that you as an Android developer continuously learn about the Android platform (and programming in general) in order to stay current. However, just as important as the nuts and bolts of programming is what to do once that incredible mobile app has been created.

Proper business planning, marketing, promotion, and advertising are the keys to success. If you are in the business of making money from your Android mobile software, the information contained within these pages is essential reading.

How to Use this Book

This book teaches you the business of Android app development, from the very genesis of your idea, all the way through ongoing support of your published app.

- **Chapter 1: "The Android Market: A Background."** The smartphone revolution has changed the way that we work and play. Android is a leader of the revolution, and this chapter discusses the history of this open-source operating system for smartphones and tablets. We also explain how Android has changed over time, and discuss porting difficulties for programs written in other coding languages.

■ **Chapter 2: "Making Sure Your App Will Succeed."** As you well know, the Android Market is flooded with applications, so you have to find out what will set yours apart from the others. We discuss what you can do to create a product that will be in demand and how to analyze the competition. A key factor is using a business plan to see and correct issues with your strategy, ensuring your app finds a market. Your business plan will involve thinking about the problem you are solving, analyzing your competition, and determining your target market. We also analyze the technical, execution, and market risks and how to price your app to succeed. At the end, we share a checklist you can use to make sure your app has what it takes!

■ **Chapter 3: "Legal Issues: Better Safe than Sorry."** An eye toward legal matters is a necessary part of the app-creation process. If you are not aware of what is at stake, you should read up on what you need to do to protect yourself legally because no one wants to be sued. We discuss personal liability; incorporation; EULAs; privacy policies; and intellectual property, which includes copyrights, trademarks, patents, licensing, and nondisclosure agreements. Like Chapter 2, it concludes with a checklist so you will be prepared!

■ **Chapter 4: "A Brief Introduction to Android Development."** As stated before, this isn't a book about programming on Android, but we do discuss the basics of programming on Android including the Eclipse IDE, the Java programming language, the Android operating system, and app deployment.

■ **Chapter 5: "Develop Apps Like a Pro."** Professional developers don't just hack code; numerous techniques and systems are also used by pros to ensure that their code is high quality. We discuss some of these techniques in this chapter. If you're a professional developer, this chapter is a basic review, but if you're new to development, it is an excellent backgrounder. We also discuss some coding tips and tricks that you can use to help you along the way.

■ **Chapter 6: "Making Money with Ads on Your Application."** Just because you are giving away an app for free doesn't mean that you can't get something out of it. Find out how to estimate revenue and what financial model to use on your application. We also discuss the types of ads that can appear on your application, including banner and full-screen. It is important to know how to understand and analyze the reporting information to better estimate revenue and uncover revenue trends.

■ **Chapter 7: "In-App Billing: Putting a Store in Your Application."** In-app purchases are yet another way for developers to make money on their Android apps, including offering user subscriptions and virtual products. This chapter describes when you will best benefit from in-app purchases and when you might want to avoid them. We also discuss numerous online stores that provide in-app purchasing capabilities. We go into particular detail of how to implement in-app purchases with Google Play and the Amazon Appstore.

■ **Chapter 8: "Making App Market Places Work for You."** As an Android developer, you have the benefit of multiple market places in which to sell your app. We show you how your marketplace listing will attract users; what screen shots to use; and how to create the appropriate icons, promotional graphics, feature graphics, and videos to promote your app. We also tell you how to beta test in the marketplace and discuss the ever-growing Amazon Appstore, among others.

■ **Chapter 9: "Getting the Word Out."** Publicity is a necessary step before getting your app out there in the world. You know the importance of publicity, but we break it down into a number of options. You should develop a plan using marketing techniques to get the word out about your app. We also discuss how to do a SWOT analysis, advertising, public relations, free publicity, Internet marketing, guerrilla marketing, trade shows, web advertising, mobile advertising, and more.

■ **Chapter 10: "After You Have a User Base."** After your app finds a user base, your job as a developer is far from done. You might want to develop a system for customer support, use Google Play Statistics, use Google Analytics, and even A/B test. All these techniques ensure that your app stays relevant and continues to fulfill the needs of your users.

The Android Market: A Background

Whenever anyone writes a book, he or she always has to be mindful of the audience. If you are an experienced Android programmer, the technical portions of this book may seem quite basic. If that is the case, we apologize in advance. We decided that because the book is about the *business* of Android apps development, some of our readers might not have any Android programming experience at all.

If you have no experience with Android, we'll try to point you in the right direction. Everyone starts with no experience at one point or another, and with technology this happens all the time. It is hard to believe that the entire idea of using a mobile "app" is less than a decade old at this writing. Ten years ago, if you were to talk about an "app" in that sense, people wouldn't be sure what you meant.

The Smartphone Revolution

If you think about all the things you do on a normal day, whether it is checking your e-mail while riding on the bus, surfing the Internet while waiting for another appointment, or running the latest application, you'll probably agree that smartphones are part of our daily life. We're sure that some of us who are Facebook and Twitter junkies wonder how in the world we lived our lives before smartphones. The technology is now something that we really take for granted, especially because most of the technology of cell phones as computers is quite new and constantly changing.

Historically speaking, the computer is a relatively new invention. The computer industry, now a giant in all types of business, is less than a century old. The Turing COLOSSUS, which was the earliest general-purpose computer developed during World War II, was designed to run aerodynamics calculations. The discoveries of Bell Telephone's transistor in 1947 and the integrated circuit, developed by Texas Instruments and Fairchild Semiconductor in 1969, helped computers make great strides during the 1950s and 1960s. Soon the IBM System/360 became the standard institutional mainframe computer. Intel co-founder Gordon Moore famously predicted that the number of components in an integrated circuit would double approximately every two years. Moore's prediction has stood the test of time, and his simple statement has since been known as Moore's Law. Because integrated circuits could do more computations for the user with less real estate, computers became smaller and smaller. The Z3 was a massive machine that took up nearly an entire building. The processing power of this gargantuan computer is minuscule compared to what we have today on the simplest of smartphones.

Through decades of advances in technology, computers became small enough to fit on a desk at home or in the office. Soon the power of the desktop transitioned to the laptop, and computers became lighter and flatter, easily transitioning from the desk to the Wi-Fi hotspot at the local coffee shop.

As computer technology improved, so did that of cellular phones, leading to a mobile phone revolution. Cellular phones were once a toy that only the rich could afford because they often cost a few thousand dollars. There were phones such as the 1983 Motorola DynaTAC 8000x, and they were a burden on their users because they weighed almost two pounds. There was a period when the weight of cell phones worked against them, but they were very popular to have in the car during the '90s. Fortunately, phones such as the 1989 Motorola MicroTAC 9800X were light enough to fit in the jacket pocket, and others, such as the Motorola StarTAC, became popular with their clamshell design.

The next logical step was to put more features on a cell phone than just phone and texting, and they soon became "smarter." Now all the power of being connected to the Internet was in the palm of one's hand. Ericsson was the first to call its phone a "smartphone," and the Nokia 9000 Communicator had similar features and was driven by an Intel 386 CPU, the same CPU previously used in Intel desktop computers.

Most tech enthusiasts remember when Steve Jobs unveiled the iPhone, a smartphone designed with the consumer in mind. We ask a lot of our tech friends, "Where were you when the iPhone was announced?" Tech enthusiasts remember when Jobs brought out his new toy, and how its one-button goodness with its "apps" changed the mobile world forever.

The rapid development of smartphone technology in the last decade is explained by Koomey's Law (somewhat similar to Moore's Law). Dr. Jonathan Koomey of Stanford University has shown that the need for electrical power (battery capacity) halves every 1.6 years. This means that computers don't just get faster (owing to greater transistor counts) but they also get smaller and more portable! Because the battery takes up less and less room on a smartphone, smartphones can pack a lot of computing power into the remaining volume.

But the computing power is only half the equation. The other half is connectivity. Smartphones are almost always online. Always-on connectivity creates amazing possibilities. The app store, a staple of all modern smartphones, is a direct outgrowth of always-on connectivity.

Now we are in an age when we can do just about anything with our phones, thanks to the app revolution. Just think about how businesses like Instagram have flourished with this new smartphone age, something that wasn't even possible a decade ago!

Every new technology creates new opportunities. As we mentioned before, the size of a computer has decreased. With this decrease in size has come a decrease in the price of computers overall. The same applies to smartphones, which are getting cheaper for the consumer thanks to contracted deals from carriers. Today, many users in countries that can't afford desktop or laptop computers have access to smartphones, with mobile networks that take them to the World Wide Web and beyond.

Though we can't go to every place in the world and get a signal, that's changing fast. In fact, even today one in three people on Earth have Internet access, and many of them have access through cellular networks.

According to the latest research from Strategy Analytics, the number of smartphones passed one billion in the third quarter of 2012. This is a mere 16 years after the first smartphones hit the market. Very few inventions have swept the globe so quickly.

This is great news for app developers. Smartphones have already changed the way we work and play, but we're sure there are many undiscovered ideas that clever app developers will unleash upon the world.

And the good news for you, dear reader, is that Android is by far the most popular smartphone operating system. In fact, in the last quarter of 2012, 70 percent of smartphone shipments were Android phones!

The Beginning of Android

A lot of people hail the iPhone as the first smartphone, but as we mentioned before, it was not. It was unique in its iOS operating system, and it may seem as if the Android operating system is a mere imitation. However, work leading to the Android OS began long before the iPhone was released to the public in 2007. Andy Rubin, known as one of the founders of Android (later acquired by Google) had been working on smartphone designs since January, 2000. The company he founded prior to Android was called Danger, Inc., which released the Hiptop (also known as the T-Mobile Sidekick) in October, 2002, years before Apple released its first smartphone.

Andy Rubin, along with Rich Miner, Nick Sears, and Chris White, then started Android, Inc. in 2003. In Rubin's words, there was tremendous potential in developing "smarter mobile devices that are more aware of its owner's location and preferences" (`http://www.businessweek.com/ stories/2005-08-16/google-buys-android-for-its-mobile-arsenal`). The company ran out of money, but it had developed an open source operating system for mobile phones by the time it was acquired by Google in 2005. Android worked rather discreetly on its mobile operating system for about two years.

Google helped start the Open Handset Alliance (OHA), which is a consortium of a lot of companies such as HTC, Motorola, Samsung, Sprint Nextel, T-Mobile, and other big names in the telecommunications industry. This group eventually unveiled the mobile operating system that we know today as Android. The first public beta of Android was released in November 2007, a mere five months after the iPhone first hit the market.

Android and iOS are currently the two major players in the world of mobile phone operating systems. Microsoft has only a fraction of the market with its Windows Phone 8 operating system, in spite of some successful flagship phones from Nokia such as the Lumia 920. The BlackBerry market was once significant, but according to comScore MobiLens, it accounts for less than six percent of the marketplace.

However, BlackBerry has recently released some new devices with a new operating system, and its fortunes might change. In a sign of how important Android has become, the new BlackBerry devices support a "Runtime for Android apps." This is a series of tools that allow you to easily repackage your existing Android apps to work on BlackBerry phones. We'll get into this in more detail later in the book, but rest assured, even if BlackBerry is wildly successful, you're making the right choice by developing for Android!

Why Android?

Android is by far the world's most widely used mobile phone operating system. If you want to reach the most users with a single code base, Android is the way. As we just mentioned, you can even easily get your app in front of BlackBerry users!

Android is quite simply crushing iPhone in user adoption rates. According to Strategy Analytics, in 2012 more than 3.5 Android smartphones shipped for every iPhone. Android has shown quite a lot of growth. In 2010, 100,000 new devices were activated each day. In 2011, 500,000 new devices were activated each day. According to Google chairman Eric Schmidt, as of April 2013 there are more than 1.5 million new Android users *every day*!

Even better, Google Play, which once lagged behind the Apple App Store in revenue, is coming into its own. Google Play revenue grew by 90 percent in the first quarter of 2013 relative to the last quarter of 2012. In the same time period, Apple's App Store revenues grew by only 25 percent. Particularly in Asia, Google Play revenue growth rates are astounding. Japan has surpassed the United States in Google Play revenue! South Korea is also incredibly strong. At these growth rates, it seems like only a matter of time before the Google Play store becomes the dominant app store. In terms of the marketplace for apps, Google Play currently has more than 700,000 applications, which have been downloaded more than 25 *billion* times!

Most successful Android application stories are pretty well known. As an example, *Angry Birds* by Rovio is free for Android users, and it is a mobile game giant that has produced massive funds for the company. The mobile game had more than two million Android downloads in the three days after its Android release, and seven million Android downloads one month after that. Rovio, the game's developer, is still finding ways to make money on the *Angry Birds* franchise with spin-offs and even merchandise.

Of course, there are more successful applications than just the ones made for gaming. For example, Edward Kim, the author of the *Car Locator* application, was initially excited to be making $20 per day. Within five months, he was making more than $13,000 per month in sales.

You will soon discover that the massive quantity of Android applications on the market can work against the developer, as the Android market is flooded with applications of all types. It's not uncommon for 20,000 new apps to appear each month.

This means that one application, as great as it might be, can get "lost in the crowd" and become very difficult to be noticed by its intended audience. Android users might pay to download one type of application even though a free one with more features is readily available. All this because some of the better applications can't get noticed in the world of many, many Android applications.

Keep in mind, however, that the Apple App Store has roughly the same number of apps as Google Play, so iOS application developers have the same problems when it comes to standing out from the crowd. Remember, unlike Apple, Google built its brand on the strength of its search abilities. You can be sure that engineers at Google are hard at work figuring out the best ways to provide Google Play users with search capabilities that let them find exactly the app they're looking for.

In fact, Roy is happy to report that searching for his apps in Google results in first page listings (see Figure 1-1).

Figure 1-1. A screen shot of the Google Play Market that shows Roy Sandberg's app

Android vs. iOS

When the iPhone was first unveiled, a new sort of business model was established for consumer electronics. Although Steve Jobs and his associates at Apple were not the first to invent the touchscreen, they were able to create a new type of software enterprise that was personable and utilitarian. Apple's "there's an app for that" slogan has promised users that the mobile software they need should be readily available where and when they need it. It works for the smartest engineer and the dumbest consumer, and it created a new type of software market. Historically, the Apple App Store has led the way by a wide margin in terms of number of apps and downloads. That, however, is set to change. The Google Play App Market has nearly reached parity with Apple, both in terms of the number of apps and the number of downloads. As of October, 2012, iOS had only 10 percent more downloads than Android.

Although iOS still has a sizable lead in terms of total revenue, that gap is also closing fast. If the trend lines continue at their current pace, Android could surpass iOS in total revenue by early 2014. In the near future, we can expect Android to take the lead in terms of total apps, app downloads, and app revenue. If we were betting types, we'd place our bets on Android!

The Difference Between Android and iOS

As a developer, you should know how Android compares to iOS at least at some level.

Apple's iOS is a proprietary operating system, while Android is open source, which gives users the right to study, change, and improve the design through ready availability of the source code. Internally, Android uses the Linux kernel.

One of the great things about Android developer tools is they are free. This is one of the reasons why the operating system is so popular on smartphones and tablets, and why it will probably have a significant presence on televisions in the near future.

Another way that Android differs from Apple is that Android has no approval process when it comes to apps placed in Google Play. Once the user has signed up, uploading and publishing becomes a relatively simple process. Remember how we mentioned earlier that the Android marketplace is crowded with many, many applications? A simpler approval process does mean that substandard applications can be prominent in the market. This is what makes a single quality app hard to notice. On the other hand, there are many app stores other than Google Play that an Android developer can select from. Many of these app stores have a more involved approval process. For example, Roy has seen very good results with the SlideMe store, which although much smaller than Google Play, currently results in more than 15 percent of the downloads for one of his apps.

Android apps are written primarily in Java, and Java is extremely well known. It is the most popular language in the langpop.com normalized comparison of computer languages. Open standards mean lots of open source. Java is the third most popular language on Google Code (langpop.com), which gives you an idea of how much new code is being written for it. Java also has the largest addressable user base of any smartphone operating system. It is easy to write, easy to test, easy to deploy, and has worldwide reach in multiple marketplaces. Both Google Play and the Amazon Appstore are thriving marketplaces for apps, and there are others that we will discuss in later chapters when we discuss putting your applications on the market.

BlackBerry applications are a new market for Android apps. It's easy to port an existing Android app (v.2.3.3 or later, with an update to Jelly Bean 4.1 forthcoming) to the BlackBerry platform.

The Android application programming interface (API) is very well documented, and most users come up to speed very quickly. In comparison, iOS is known to have a steeper learning curve. iOS applications are usually written using Objective C, which is rarely used outside of iOS development. In comparison, Java is a very well-known language, which makes Android easy to learn for existing Java developers.

For example, Roy knew some basic Java before writing his first app, and he was able to write a complex multithreaded application in only a few weeks. Most of the learning curve relates to the Android application life cycle, which is rather different from PC or server-side Java programming. But once you understand this life cycle, it promotes easy code reuse and allows you to tap into the power of applications written by other developers. The Android application life cycle also promotes the development of energy-efficient applications that "play nicely with others."

But the ways that the Android ecosystem makes app development easy extend past the logistics of programming. As a novice developer, Roy was also impressed with the ease with which he was able to access an international market. His first commercial app, the Sandberg Sound BPM Detector, allows a user to determine the beats per minute of any song it hears. It's used by both DJs and musicians around the world. With a few clicks, Roy was able to deploy the app worldwide. What's even more impressive is that written text describing the app was automatically translated to dozens of languages. Users who have no knowledge of English see Roy's apps listed in their native language, and the apps can display their text in the user's native language as well. Similarly, the Android ecosystem takes care of the logistics of international banking and purchasing. Once Roy selected an app's price in U.S. dollars, Android automatically suggested pricing in native currencies around the world. Even though his apps are listed in 190 countries around the world, purchases appear in his bank account in U.S. dollars, without any intervention on his part. Such is the power of Android.

Free third-party tools also make Android easier to use, even for non-Java programmers. Scripting Layer for Android (SL4A) allows Ruby, Python, Perl, JavaScript, and a number of other interpreted languages to run on an Android device. They have access to most of the Android API and don't require a developer to follow the application life cycle. If your app is best implemented as a simple script, this might be the way to go. Currently SL4A is in alpha, but it has been under development for many years.

If you're a Ruby programmer, you could check out Ruboto (`www.ruboto.org`). Ruboto uses the JRuby compiler (which translates Ruby to Java virtual machine code) to convert Ruby language code into Android application code. Because JRuby supports just-in-time (JIT) compilation, Ruby code generated by Ruboto is quite fast.

So we think Android is the easier platform to develop on. But don't just take our word for it. In a *Developer Economics 2013 Survey* of 1,200 app developers who develop for both iOS and Android, the majority stated that Android development had both an easier learning curve and a lower development cost than iOS.

Versions of Android

Android got off to a slow start with the HTC Dream (also known as the T-Mobile G1). Since then, Android has been gaining popularity with the release of every new version. It is important that you know about them when you begin developing Android applications because newer versions contain more features than their predecessors. In terms of programming, these versions have a definite numerical designation. We will discuss that when we get into downloading Android development tools like Android SDK and Eclipse. For now, you should know that in addition to the version number, versions also have an informal name that is always a sweet treat. This cute tradition began with version 1.5.

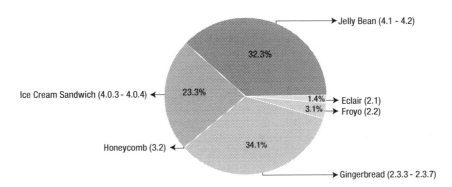

Figure 1-2. Percentage of the Android universe using each platform version

Here is a very basic summary of some the latest versions of Android:

- Version 1.5 (Cupcake):
    - Allows for video recording through camcorder
    - Bluetooth enabling
    - Widgets on homescreen
    - Allows for animated screen
    - Uploading of YouTube videos and Picasa photos "on the fly"
- Version 1.6 (Donut):
    - Features a camcorder, camera, and Integrated Gallery
    - Voice Search
    - Voice Dial
    - Bookmark
    - History
    - Contacts Search
    - WVGA screen resolution
    - Comes with Google turn-by-turn navigation
- Version 2.0/2.1 (Éclair):
    - HTML5 and Exchange Active Sync 2.5 support
    - Improved speed
    - Google Maps 3.1.2
    - MS Exchange Server Integration
    - Flash for Camera
    - Bluetooth 2.1 integration
    - Option of virtual keyboard
- Version 2.2 (Froyo):
    - Screen is 320dpi with 720p
    - JIT compiler
    - Chrome with JavaScript Engine version 8
    - Wi-Fi hotspot tethering
    - Bluetooth contacts sharing
    - Adobe Flash support for version 10.1
    - Apps can be installed on expandable memory like SDcard

- Version 2.3 (Gingerbread):
  - Improved gaming graphics and audio effects
  - SIP VoIP support
  - WXGA (Xtra large screen size and resolution)
  - Near field communication
  - Copy-Paste feature
  - Download manager for large downloads
  - Better control of applications
  - Support for multiple cameras
- Version 3.0, 3.1, and 3.2 (Honeycomb):
  - The first tablet-only release
  - 3-D Desktop with newer widgets
  - Tabbed web browsing and "incognito" mode for anonymous browsing
  - Google talk Video Chat
  - Hardware acceleration
  - Multicore processor support
  - Multipane navigation
- Version 4 (Ice Cream Sandwich):
  - Streamlined user interface fit for both tablets and smartphones
  - Advanced App framework
  - Facial recognition
  - Better voice recognition
  - Web browser with up to 16 tabs
  - Resizable widgets
- Version 4.1 and 4.2 (Jelly Bean):
  - Google Now
  - Voice Search
  - Android Beam
  - Speed enhancements
  - Camera App enhancements with HDR
- Version 5 (Key Lime Pie):
  - At present, we don't know much about the features here; perhaps later versions will keep us updated.

You will discover that specific Android devices start out as one particular version of Android, and upgrades tend to come out slowly for certain devices. This is because Android releases a new version, and then hardware vendors and cellular carriers modify the source to meet their needs. In fact, the cellular carrier might not even update older phones with a new version of Android even though the hardware is most certainly capable of it.

The Challenges of Working with Android

We have already mentioned that some of the great things about Android developer tools is they are free, and that Android differs from Apple in that the official Google Play marketplace has no approval process when it comes to apps. Once the user has signed up, uploading and publishing becomes a relatively simple process.

While Android apps are both relatively easy to develop and easy to deploy, there is no guarantee that your app will work perfectly on every Android device. You can imagine users who have a phone that your application won't work on. You won't be getting a recommendation from them!

Typical problems can include simple things like failure to format correctly for different screen sizes. Even if you follow all the best practices, sometimes a phone uses a strange resolution. Your app might still work, but the layout might be unpleasant to the user, resulting in a bad review.

It's possible to test different screen resolutions using the free Android phone emulator. But this emulator often runs too slowly for computationally expensive applications. Moreover, there are a few bugs in the emulator that can cause certain apps to behave incorrectly when emulated. Although the emulator is good for simple testing, it isn't foolproof.

Another common issue concerns Android phones with different hardware capabilities. Not all phones have forward-facing cameras, for example. Some phones don't have the "horsepower" for computationally expensive graphics. Every hardware manufacturer is free to add custom features and capabilities to its phone, which means not every phone provides every feature. Android provides the developer with ways to ensure that the phone has the features you need, but these sorts of differences between hardware platforms are one of the major challenges of programming for Android. The iPhone is a phone, but Android is a true operating system, supporting hundreds of unique devices from dozens of manufacturers.

As a developer, you should always think about how to write an app in the way that reaches the most users. Often, you are better off using an older version of Android than you prefer and avoiding the latest snazzy hardware features. This lets you reach more users. Android has an enormous installed base of users, but few of them are using the latest version.

If you get serious about Android development, you may want to buy a used Android phone or two in addition to your primary phone (which we assume is an Android phone!). Developing an app that runs on older versions of Android ensures that you can address the majority of the market. The only sure way to know whether your app works well on multiple versions is to test them. If you're committed to developing quality apps, you will want to test your app on at least a few different handsets.

Another option, if you can afford it, is to use a service like www.perfectomobile.com/, which allows you to test against hundreds of real Android phones using a cloud-based interface.

Porting Difficulties

For those who want to turn their iOS app into a full-fledged Android application (or vice versa), we want to let you know the process and pitfalls. If you're only focusing on the Android market, you can safely skip this section. However, many developers aim to develop for both Android and iOS in order to maximize their revenue. We will cover how to do that by the end of this chapter.

Let's say you've written an iOS app that is out right now or perhaps waiting in the app approval process. To turn it into an Android application, you have to adapt your software so that an executable program can be created for a computing environment that is different from the one that it was originally designed for. This is known as *porting*.

iOS apps are generally written in Objective-C, while Android apps are generally written in Java. Although the logic of these programming languages is quite similar because they are both linear, procedural, and use notions of object orientation (OO), they are very different with respect to OS support, GUI objects, and application life cycle. Sadly, Objective-C is not supported on Android.

As far as we know, there isn't any magical program that will allow you to put iPhone apps in and get Android applications out (unless you use development tools that have this in mind from the beginning). We will talk about cross-platform development tools later, but first we'll explain what you can do for both Android and iOS.

Although your iOS coding can't be reused for Android coding, you don't have to rewrite all your Android code from scratch. For example, you can completely reuse the icons and images, as well as any SQLite database code. Additionally, certain types of C code in an iPhone app (for example, code for image processing or digital signal processing) may be directly utilized in Android using the Android Native Development Kit (NDK). Although you might think that the user interface (UI) design would be reusable, iOS and Android have different UI elements, and forcing an Android app to behave like an iPhone app can be a time-consuming (and costly) endeavor. In some situations, you may be able to reuse use cases that were written for iOS apps, but you should consider the impact that the Android UI has on your use cases. Also, the Android ecosystem tends to favor free apps with advertising or in-app purchasing more than iOS does. In other words, a change to the overall business plan might be in order when porting to Android.

It usually takes nearly the same amount of effort to port an iOS app to Android as it does to create it. It really depends on how big the application is, as well as the complexity of the code, reliance on GUI tools, and ability of the developer.

By the way, there are people who make it their business to program apps, and that could lighten your workload. Since your app already exists in one form, it's easy to outsource application porting; the developer can always use the original app as a reference.

If you have written your iOS app in ANSI C or C++, perhaps using one of the many gaming engines that are designed for that purpose, then your task may be simplified. Android has the NDK, which allows for ANSI C or C++ code to be called from the Android Java code and vice versa.

Examples of Cross-Platform Development Tools

Chances are you want your application to be downloaded as much as possible, which means you probably want it to be on as many devices as possible. If you want to have your application on both iOS and Android as well as other mobile platforms, you may want to use one of the cross-platform development kits.

Although we believe that the application market is headed toward a universal solution, we are not quite there yet. This book focuses on the Android Software Development Kit (Android SDK) for constructing Android applications. For completeness, however, we will discuss a few cross-platform development kits, just so you know there are alternatives.

LiveCode

LiveCode is the work of RunRev, a company that creates development tools. In the words of Ben Beaumont, product manager for RunRev, LiveCode is "a multi-platform element environment that [has] now been moved to the mobile space." LiveCode was originally made for Mac, Windows, and Linux, and it boasts "compile-free coding." Compile-free coding means that when you make a change to your program, you will see it as you are programming. This is different from the usual method of editing, compiling, running, and debugging.

LiveCode also has a visual development environment in which the user can drag and drop the objects and images that will make up the final interface. The user can then attach scripts to these objects to really bring them to life as well as lend them speed. LiveCode uses a very high-level language, which allows the user to write in code that is very close to English. This allows users to write in this code easily, and the code will be easier to read. All this enables the creation of live prototypes that actually run on the device, and promises to make it easy to quickly iterate and improve your application, because you can immediately see the results of your work.

Appcelerator

Titanium has created a free and open source application development platform that allows the user to create native mobile, tablet, and desktop application experiences. Its Appcelerator program allows the user to build applications full of features, as if they were written in Objective-C or Java. The end results are native apps that are customizable with a lot of features, all built with the web technology of JavaScript.

Appcelerator allows developers to concentrate on building the application and provides a toolset for many platforms.

appMobi XDK

The appMobi mobile app development XDK is made for web developers, and it claims that if you can build an application for the web using HTML5, CSS3, and JavaScript, then you can build it as an application on the iPhone, the iPad, and Android smartphones and pads. According to appMobi, developers can develop robust, 100 percent native API–compliant mobile applications in hours using preferred editors, and write once and deploy to all target platforms.

The XDK includes an onscreen emulator with simple, approachable tool palettes to simulate user interaction with a testing device. It also allows you to send your application project over a local Wi-Fi connection or upload it to the cloud to test it from anywhere.

Note   You will need Java 6 and Google Chrome 6.0 to run the appMobi mobile app development XDK.

appMobi also offers a service known as MobiUs, which allows any app publisher to offer its app from anywhere on the Web. This could mean the end of frustrating and complicated processes of submission and approval to traditional app distributors (and also the end of developers needing to share their profits with these distributors). It is also cloud-based, which means it is possible to create iPhone apps on a Windows PC and Android applications on a Mac.

PhoneGap

According to its web site, PhoneGap allows users to build apps with web standards based on HTML 5.0. PhoneGap users can also access native APIs to create applications for multiple platforms, including iOS, Android, Windows, BlackBerry, webOS, and more. PhoneGap is currently in version 1.0.0.

Summary

The Android application market has grown rapidly in the past few years. In the near future, it is likely to eclipse the Apple App Store and become the largest source of revenue for app developers. However, there are so many Android applications on the market that a developer really has to have something very different and outstanding to achieve significant revenue. Beyond that, merely having a great app isn't enough. You have to make sure your app connects with the right users, and you have to make sure your business case is sound.

Let's see how to make your app stand out from the crowd and reach the right users with a compelling business case.

Chapter 2

Making Sure Your App Will Succeed

We're sure you have heard the old cliché about how "Rome wasn't built in a day." If you want to build a successful application, it might take several days, months, or even years, depending on its complexity. However, we're also sure Rome was not built without some sort of plan in mind, and if you want to build your app empire, you will need a business plan that takes into account the obstacles along the way of app-building.

Your App and a Business Plan

A *business plan* is a document that states the goals for a business, why those goals are attainable, and how those goals can be achieved. There is no one set template for a business plan. If you are planning to raise venture capital, you will want to consider a more formal approach than we are going to suggest. However, most app developers won't need to raise capital. So we're going to stick to an informal sort of business plan to help you vet your idea.

Why should you have a business plan? Perhaps the better question is this: what will happen if you don't have a business plan?

We explained in Chapter 1 that the Android world is booming. There may be hundreds of millions of Android users, but in a world with hundreds of thousands of apps, it's hard for one app to stand out from the crowd.

While Android makes it easy to develop and publish your app, the bad news is that it is unlikely to have significant sales without a carefully thought out and executed plan. A business plan will give you critical insights into whether your application can succeed in the current Android market.

Perhaps you doubt whether you are smart enough to create a business plan and don't think you can foresee the conditions that will affect your Android application until it is too late. Yes, it is impossible to foresee every possible variable that could affect the success of your application, but that's exactly why you need a business plan!

The biggest benefit of writing a business plan is that the process forces you to think deeply about what exactly you are trying to accomplish. You get out of the process only what you put into it, so don't just skim over the next few paragraphs; open a text editor and start taking notes about how this specifically applies to *your* app.

Because you are probably not writing a business plan to submit to investors, we will focus on the key factors that will help you see critical issues before you even start writing code. We'll call this condensed, simplified business plan a *mini-business plan*. Let's break it down into seven parts:

1. Identify the problem that you are solving.

2. Analyze your competition.

3. Determine the target market.

4. Evaluate technical, execution, and market risks.

5. Think about monetization and pricing.

6. Estimate a schedule.

7. Test your market demand hypothesis.

Think of the business plan as the oven that bakes your app idea to completion. Don't start coding until you're sure your idea isn't half-baked! Entrepreneurs (and writers) inevitably find themselves making an *elevator pitch*, which is a capsulized way of pitching an idea as quickly as the duration of an elevator ride. Hopefully, you can get your audience interested by the time the door opens on their floor. As you work on your business plan, ask yourself how you would "elevator pitch" your idea to your customers. This is a good gut check for your business plan.

Identify the Problem That You Are Solving

Here is the first rule about a developing a decent application: a good app solves a problem. The question you should ask yourself is this: what can my app bring to the world? Even the simplest, easy-to-learn games can cure the user of boredom, and a few levels of *Angry Birds* have made bus rides or waits in long lines go by a lot more quickly.

Is your app a vitamin or a pain-killer? Vitamins are "nice-to-have" solutions that one takes if they remember, but no one will ever run to in desperation. Pain-killers are the "have-to-have" applications—the ones that we buy a smartphone or tablet to use.

If you have an Android device, we suggest taking it out and scrolling through the applications that you have. Chances are that most of your recently used apps are pain-killers. The vitamins are often those apps that you downloaded on a whim, but hardly ever use.

Clearly, our advice is to write an application that is a pain-killer rather than a vitamin. While gaming apps are often vitamins, there are exceptions. The entertainment market can be fickle, but some forms of entertainment are more of a pain-killer than others. If you are like Mark, you might even be addicted to gaming apps. You can benefit from considering what problem your game might solve. For example, will your game still be fun if played in short sessions? If so, it solves the problem of short periods of boredom. Some games take a while to learn, and they might require a few hours before a user truly enjoys them. You wouldn't want to advertise a game like that on a local bus line.

Analyze Your Competition

Every idea, no matter how original, must compete with other ideas for mindshare. It is good to know who your competition is before you set your app free in the world. *If you can't figure out who your competition is, you're flying blind.*

Imagine if you built some sort of transporter that worked just like the ones in *Star Trek*. You might think this idea is so original and important that it would dominate the market, making a competitive analysis unnecessary. But what if it costs $10,000 per use? Even if the transporter can safely and instantly get people to their destination, most people would still pick their favorite airline (or their cars) for their domestic travel. But a competitive analysis would reveal that long-distance first class business travel costs about the same, so that might be the best market to target.

Similarly, no one will want to use an application if there is already one on the market that does the same thing (and, in some cases, does it better) at a lower price (or for free). In the world of apps, this problem is even more acute than in other competitive environments. Popular apps appear higher up in the Google Play listings, so existing favorites tend to become entrenched. You have to ask why someone would use your application instead of a similar and competing application. Unless your application is better, you will not displace the long-time favorites. In order to succeed, you have to do what your competition is doing *significantly* better. Otherwise, you might want your application to do something else.

There are many ways to learn about your competition, but at the very least you should be searching the app stores for apps in your category. Read the reviews, try them out, and ask your friends to give you feedback. You could even conduct a survey. You should also think more broadly about your competition. Is there PC software that does something similar? What about an electronic gadget? Your first goal is to get a sense of what is out there.

After you have collected some raw data, the best way to analyze your competition is to make a chart called a competitor array. This chart should rank your business along with your competitors using a number of factors. The factors are specific to your industry, but you can find a simplified example of a competitor array in Table 2-1. Two turn-by-turn navigation apps are being compared on four factors. Notice that the factors are weighted. It is up to you to decide which factors are most important, thereby deriving the appropriate weighting. Once you compile this information, it can inform your decision making regarding changes you will need to make before your app is competitive.

Table 2-1. *Using a Competitor Array to Rank Two Mobile Navigation Apps*

CompetitiveFactor Analysis	Weighting	My App Rating	My App Weighted	Competitor B Rating	Competitor B Weighted
1 – Accuracy of Directions	.4	6	2.4	3	1.2
2 – Latency of Turn-By-Turn Navigation	.3	4	1.2	5	1.5
3 – Cost	.2	3	.6	3	.6
4 – Server Latency	.1	7	.7	4	.4
Totals	**1.0**	**20**	**4.9**	**15**	**3.7**

Determine the Target Market

You might be concerned that your app will never stack up against the competition. Don't worry! We're not saying that you have to create a new application category to succeed. Ideally, you will find a target market that isn't being adequately served by your competitors. By targeting that market exclusively, you can appeal to customers who are being ignored by your competition.

If your analysis ends up being wrong, and the target market isn't working out, don't despair! Often, with minor changes, you can focus your existing app on a new part of the market your competitors aren't concentrating on. Either way, by targeting a specific niche, your app will show up earlier in searches specific to that submarket. You can then market your app as designed for that particular submarket. In the previous example, suppose that the other mobile navigation apps had limited capability to be used by bicyclists. Perhaps you could add features targeting the specific issues faced by bicyclists. That would make your app the ideal solution, even if other turn-by-turn navigation apps had much better performance for car drivers.

Let's talk about how to determine your target market. You will discover that very few things have universal appeal. Think about the films that you love, and you can probably find a person or group of people who hate them. If you are smart, you will discover what kind of person will like your application even before it is created.

Ideally, you want your product to be used by everyone, but this rarely happens in the real world. It usually turns out that there is some particular market segment or culture that makes heavy use of a product. Advertisers realize that and often cater their commercials or other forms of advertising to this crowd. Think about all the ads you have seen, from the Super Bowl million-dollar ads to local low-budget ads: they are always targeted to a specific crowd. If you can figure out what type of person will be more likely to use your application, you have taken the first step of finding your target audience.

In other words, there is probably a specific type of crowd, whether scrapbookers, stamp collectors, sports nuts, or any other type of enthusiast who would probably consume your Android application more eagerly than the average consumer. This could be the most important question to consider when deciding how to market your Android application.

As mentioned before, the Google Play marketplace has hundreds of thousands of Android applications, so it takes a lot to make one in particular stand out. Think about how much time and money it will take to reach your audience. If it takes more money to reach them than you expect to make, you have a problem. We will explain exactly how to reach your audience in Chapter 9.

In short, you should determine to whom you are selling. Put yourself in the customers' shoes, and imagine what they're looking for. Does narrowing your target group make it easier to reach them? Does narrowing your target group make it easier to focus on their needs? Narrowing your market isn't a bad thing; it has many marketing advantages, and becoming a niche product is also a great way to stand out from the competition.

In fact, most professional venture capitalists become worried when they hear that a company is pursuing more than one market. It's just too hard to focus on more than one type of customer when you're first starting out. If you have identified more than one target audience, you should strongly consider just picking the best one of the bunch and focusing your initial efforts there.

Of course, you might worry that your target market is too small, but be sure you are thinking about market size correctly. Say you are working on an app that lets people tune their kazoos. You would probably assume that the number of kazoo-playing Android users is fairly small. But that's actually an incorrect approach when thinking about the market. The question isn't how many kazoo-toting Android users there are; the question is how many you can reach and how much they would be willing to pay for a kazoo-tuning app. Imagine, for example, that there is a thriving kazoo special interest forum that nearly every kazoo player frequents and it publicly laments the lack of kazoo-tuning apps. In that scenario, you might actually have a very good market because it's easy to reach. Nearly every kazoo user would learn about your app if you posted there.

On the other hand, you might have a great app for people with cars, but have no way to let most of them know about it. Considering that more than 95 percent of all American households own a car, it would seem that your target market is large enough. But that high potential audience does not necessarily mean a huge number of users. Do not ignore the difficulty of letting potential users know about your app. Creating an app with a really clever feature is often enough to capture the interest of journalists, and that allows you to reach users for free. We'll talk more about that in Chapter 9.

Let's talk about some factors you can consider when imagining what your target market might look like. Naturally, you could start by thinking about basic demographics, which might include things like age, location, gender, income level, education level, marital status, occupation, and ethnic background. These factors can create an impression of a specific customer in your mind, but it's going to be very fuzzy.

Try to imagine your target customers in even greater detail. Think about personal characteristics such as their personality, attitudes, values, interests, hobbies, lifestyle, and general behavior. Keep thinking about this until you can imagine an archetypal customer. Is there an acquaintance you know or a TV character that fits this description? Keep that image in mind.

Now imagine how your app will be used by your archetypal customers. How and when do you imagine they would use your app? What aspect of your application would they consider to be the most important? How will you reach out to them? Do they read newspapers or are they Facebook users? Are they members of some sort of organization you could contact?

Now that you've narrowed your vision of your customer, make sure that your market is large enough. Remember, sometimes it's less about the absolute size of the market, and more about your ability to reach them. But certainly there has to be enough people in the world to fit your description so that you can reach your revenue goals. Of course, you need to be sure that your archetypal customer can afford your app! And finally, you need to be able to reach them via some marketing technique.

Evaluate Technical, Execution, and Market Risks

Any time you want to do something, there is a risk. With every risk, there is a chance of failure, which is a word we hate to hear, especially when our name is associated with it. We'll let you in on a little secret: fail fast. Evaluating risks ahead of time is a great way to determine where you might fail. You can then decide whether the risks can be managed; if not, you can cut your losses early.

There are three reasons why you might fail:

- Technical risk
- Execution risk
- Market risk

We'll examine each of these risks in the following sections.

Technical Risk

Technical risk is the simple question of whether something can be done using the technology and tools that Android provides. Hopefully, the technology is capable of doing what you want it to do, but some apps push the limits. If you are writing a very computationally expensive app (one that really hogs the processor), you should pay careful attention to this risk. Slower Android phones might not even be able to run your app, and even the fastest phones will experience significant battery drain if your app runs continuously. You might find similar technical risks when streaming large amounts of data over the network. You should ask yourself whether slower network connections will be able to handle your application. Other areas of technical risk include microphone sensitivity, speaker loudness, and insufficient screen real estate or resolution. On a more general level, some algorithms simply can't be made to work in all cases. For example, very large vocabulary speech recognition systems often run into problems. Visual object recognition apps might get confused with certain objects. These sorts of issues need to be ironed out early in the development process to avoid lots of wasted time and money.

If you have identified areas of technical risk, you should make sure to get a handle on these areas before writing the full-fledged app. A simple prototype or even crude hacked-up software can often give you a much better sense of whether the idea will work. Always strive to eliminate risk in your business plan!

Execution Risk

Execution risk is a simple matter of whether you can accomplish what you set out to do. For example, maybe your app calls for very complicated algorithms, but you are a novice programmer. Maybe your app won't succeed without high-quality graphics, but you're not an experienced graphic designer. Your app might be technically feasible, but you might lack the ability to implement it without huge schedule delays. If you are a novice programmer, you should really get an expert to weigh in on your plans. If you don't have ready access to an expert, Roy, one of the authors, is always happy to hear from fellow entrepreneurs. Even if he can't help you himself, he might know someone who can. You can contact him through his web site (`www.sandbergsound.com`). Remember, often the things that seem easy only look that way because we know so little about the details.

Market Risk

Market risk is essentially figuring out whether the market will use your app in the volumes you need to succeed. A very common problem faced by app developers is not being able to afford the cost of advertising. If you're selling your app for $1.00, but it costs $1.05 in advertising to make a customer, you've got a problem. Although the cost of advertising varies depending on the medium you use (Google, Facebook, magazines, TV, radio, and so on), you can make a back-of-the-envelope calculation by assuming it will cost a few cents (nominally $0.05) to reach a reader via print media. You can roughly estimate the same cost to direct a click to your web site. How many views or clicks will result in a sale? Well, that's impossible to say in advance, but if you have to guess, you shouldn't guess more than about 1 percent.

Fortunately, you don't have to guess. Offer your product for sale on your web site and record the number of unique visitors who express a willingness to pay (they hit the Buy button). You don't need to have your product ready to do this; just record the would-be buyers' contact info and tell them you'll let them know when the product is ready. We'll get into other ways of acquiring users besides advertising in Chapter 9, but you should ensure that you have a strategy for reaching your audience.

What you *shouldn't* do is think this way: "if I build it, they will come." That might work for baseball fields, but it definitely doesn't work for apps. Placing your app in the Google Play store might result in some people installing it, but you won't get enough users for even modest success without resorting to additional measures. One way to approach this problem is to think about the interests of your users and how to use those interests to reach out to them. Is there an online forum in which they congregate? Do they read certain magazines? Can you reach them using a viral technique (friends of friends)? In short, if you can't figure out how to reach out to your customers, you won't have a whole lot of them.

Think About Monetization and Pricing

A critical step in any business is pricing your offering. Customers always want to get something for nothing, and there are many applications on Android that you can get for free. As a developer, you can still make money with free apps by hosting ads. Or you can charge for your app. In fact, there are a number of options available. It's time for you to consider those options and evaluate which choice makes the most sense for your app.

Paid Apps

You can just sell your application outright, and your application has a clear price tag. Remember that most marketplaces take 30 percent of your listed price as their commission. You will have to convince customers to shell out their money on the strength of your product's description and reviews, which is a difficult thing to accomplish without marketing. You can forget whatever dream you have about putting your application on Google Play and sitting back and watching as your profits rise. On the bright side, you don't really have to update your app very frequently because after users buy it, you don't need to keep their interest; there is no additional money to be made from them. Of course, you do want your users to give you a good review, so it pays (and it's in your best interest) to ensure that your application runs at a high level of quality without any bugs.

The difficulty is constantly exposing new users to your app. Although you'll definitely get some users who find the app when they search for the right keywords, in general you'll need to find ongoing sources of publicity in order to continue generating real revenue. For lower-cost apps, advertising might not work unless your cost to acquire a new user is very low. If your app is very specialized and can support a high price (say $10 or more), you can expect some success through traditional advertising channels.

Free Apps

There might be no such thing as a free lunch, but there *is* such a thing as a free app. Most of us don't give away something for free unless we get something in return, however. So even if the users might not be paying for the privilege of running your application, it is possible to make money on it with advertisements.

You need to find a service that will pay you to put ads in your application. Usually you get paid each time a user clicks an ad. We will discuss this more in Chapter 6.

In contrast with paid applications, you are likely to get many more downloads of free applications, easily ten times as many or more. Unfortunately, you will typically make less money from each user, at least in the short term. An ad-serving company (such as Google AdMob) will serve a new ad periodically, perhaps every minute, although this is adjustable by the developer. Because any ad might be the one that interests the user of your app, the more ads your application serves, the more likely you are to get a click. What this means is that applications that the user will interact with for a long time are well-suited to the free, advertisement-backed model. In contrast, if your app solves a very important problem, but is only used once or rarely, you are probably better off making it a paid app.

Freemium Apps

A freemium app is a light version of your application that encourages users to pay for an upgrade. The free version can even run ads. If you use this model, it should be clear to the user at what point he or she will need to pay for the upgrade. Don't disguise your app as being free and later surprise your user.

Of course, this can get complicated because you have to have two versions of the same application, which means two applications need to be submitted to Google Play.

It can be difficult to determine where the cut-off point is between the free version and the paid version. *Angry Birds* made its money because the free version had a few levels, but they were enough to leave players begging for more. This is ideal; you switch from free to paid when the users are hooked. That's when they are more willing to part with their money.

Beyond that, simply building users' trust with your free app makes them more likely to feel comfortable enough with you to upgrade to the paid version. The key is that the paid version should deliver a feature that users really want after they start using the app. You can often artificially limit some capability in the free version, so it's useful, but not quite enough for power users.

Services

This technique gets the users to pay for a particular service when they download your app. You, the developer, may not even be the person providing the service, but you might make a certain amount from the service provider for each time you connect a customer.

There might be a subscription involved, such as several applications on the Kindle Fire. The Kindle Fire has a place for magazine subscriptions, but some periodicals, books, and even shows choose to be an app that one subscribes to get the latest "issue."

As this example illustrates, this monetization technique works best when the app is being used as a vehicle to deliver some underlying capability, such as frequently updated content. Because app users are very price-conscious, you need to convince them they're getting more than a mere app. Few users would agree to pay an ongoing monthly fee for an app that doesn't provide real-world value.

In-app Purchasing

In-app purchasing involves getting a user to pay for certain features within the application. This is big in games, where characters pay for larger guns, or even something seemingly superficial such as different costumes. Another example is a translation app that is free, but forces you to pay for certain language modules.

In effect, this monetization strategy is very similar to the freemium model in that the user gets the app for free and is then convinced to pay for more features. The advantage of in-app purchases is that a user could conceivably make multiple purchases over time; so for apps that get repeated use, this could result in a continuous revenue stream from purchases.

Other Models of Moneymaking

Some of the best business models involve creative monetization strategies. If you think about it, some mobile applications are just a means to implement a business transaction. eBay, for example, offers a free application that is helpful for checking on the status of auctions. Anyone who has an auction on eBay is paying eBay a small percentage; that's the heart of its business plan. The eBay application is helpful for on-the-go auctioning; it pays for itself by enabling more users to buy and sell items more easily, which means more auction purchases occur.

Flywheel, Lyft, and Uber make money by giving users a way to hail transportation (taxis, shared rides, or town cars) from their Android phones. The users don't pay to download it, there are no ads, and there are no services to pay for. So how do they make money? They charge the drivers for each fare they pick up! Often, if you can insert your app between a buyer and a seller, you can charge sellers a small fee, and they'll gladly pay it because you've brought them a customer.

Although marketplace in-app purchasing libraries don't support the sale of physical goods (see Chapter 7), you can certainly link to physical goods from within your app. Whether this is via an affiliate program (see Chapter 6) or just by a link to a product on your web site, you can certainly leverage your app as a way to promote the sale of physical goods.

Estimate a Schedule

As we explained in Chapter 1, the Android open–source development tools are completely free. But as the proverb says, time is money. Sure, you could spend a lot of time making the perfect app, but who will pay you to do it? Also, if you do create this perfect app, what if someone else is doing the same thing? Take the time to create a project schedule so you know how much time it will take; it will give you a better idea of whether it's worth your effort to get started.

You don't have to use complicated charts or special software to make a schedule, although you can if you want. The important point here is to take your idea and break it down into a series of steps. Then take those steps and break them down further. When each step takes no more than a day to implement, you have a decent schedule.

If you don't know how long something will take, you have identified an execution risk (as discussed previously). You should reach out to experts and see if you can get an estimate from them. They should be able to break down the problem into a series of steps; if they can't, they're not the experts they say they are. You can also have them estimate how long it would take to implement a solution for you and how much it would cost. This can help you decide if you have a realistic grasp of the complexities involved.

In many cases, you can write some pseudocode for your app and get a pretty decent idea of the implementation complexity by breaking down each subroutine as far as you can and estimating the lines of code per routine.

Bill Gates said, "Measuring software productivity by lines of code is like measuring progress on an airplane by how much it weighs." So it's controversial to even bring it up, but some programmers like to estimate that they can write 80 lines of quality code per day (fully tested, including unit tests). In some cases, that might help you better estimate your schedule.

Your schedule shouldn't be limited to just coding, though. You should also consider the time it will take to develop content for a web site (discussed later in this chapter and also in Chapter 9). Time spent on marketing and sales tasks should also be included. As you learn more about these topics, you can revisit your schedule.

Even fairly complicated project schedules can be written down on paper or implemented with a word processor or spreadsheet. However, if you are new to project management and want to manage your schedule in a professional manner, you should consider using project management software. At a minimum, project management software allows you to schedule your tasks so that the task duration is automatically calculated, including days off. Complicated schedules with lots of moving parts will benefit the most from this sort of software. Microsoft Project is practically the industry standard software package for project management. Fortunately, you don't need to invest in an expensive Microsoft product to get started.

ProjectLibre is a free open-source alternative to Microsoft Project that runs on Windows, Mac, and Linux. It offers many of the same features available in Microsoft Project and has user groups all over the world where you can get help. You can learn more at its official web site: `http://www.projectlibre.org/`

Testing Your Market Demand Hypothesis

There is really no way to test the success of an application without actually making, marketing, and distributing the application. If only there were some way to put a fake app out there and see how many people download it. Sadly, that is unethical, and you would receive terrible reviews and possibly get kicked out of App Stores as well as the Android developer program.

Yes, it just isn't worth that risk. However, you can do the next best thing by setting up a web site that offers your app for sale. You'll let visitors know your app isn't ready yet, but only after you gauge their reactions. If it turns out that there isn't enough demand for your app, you've saved yourself a lot of trouble, and you can just tell the folks who signed up that the project was canceled. Your web site can be designed easily and at no cost with online tools. We discuss how to quickly set up your web site later in this chapter.

Make sure that your web site includes a detailed description of your app, including (faked) screen shots if at all possible. There are a number of online tools that provide a quick and free way to prototype your user interface (UI), and your work doesn't go to waste because you'll use what you made later. We will discuss these tools in the next section.

When writing the description and making the screen shots, you should be answering several questions:

- What assumptions have you made in the previous sections of your business plan that you can test?
- Can your description be narrowly focused on your target market?
- Can your screen shot suggest the monetization strategy?

Beyond having a detailed description with screen shots, it's very important that you offer the reader an option to download the app. This option should also list the price of the app if it isn't free. By simulating the actual market conditions that real users would experience, you screen out people who are merely curious and focus on real prospects.

When users try to download the app, you should direct them to a signup page. This page tells them that the app isn't yet available, but they'll be contacted as soon as it is. If you include a field to allow them to leave comments, you have a great way to get feedback from potential users. This is easy to do with the free web site building tools that we will discuss in the following section.

After your hypothesis-testing web site is ready, you need to get some eyeballs to it. This is where your initial work defining your target audience first becomes useful. You figured out how to reach your audience, right? So post something on one of the (many) forums where your potential users hang out, and get a few of them to visit your page. You don't need many, but you do want to keep track of how many people out there read your post, how many of them clicked through to your web site, and how many reached the signup page. This will give you an idea of how popular your app is with the target audience.

If you have more than one target audience that you're deciding on, repeating this process for each audience is a great way to pick the winner based on hard data. After you get some percentages figured out, you can determine how many users you will get when you scale up and reach out to a bigger audience.

The feedback alone makes this process worth it. It is one thing to have an idea, but quite another when real people are telling you what they think about your idea. Often, you'll find that you understand your target audience a lot better simply by reading a few comments they have sent you. Use all this information to determine whether you have what it takes to succeed. Remember, often the idea you start off with changes dramatically after you make contact with your intended target audience. Whatever you do, be certain that you're listening to your potential customers. Their opinions are the ones that matter.

Tools for Prototyping Your Screen Shots

When testing your market demand hypothesis, it's important that your screen shots look as realistic as possible. Fortunately, there are many tools you can use to prototype screen shots. If you determine that your app's future is promising, the work you put into screen shots will be time well spent. In some cases, these prototyping tools can generate usable Android XML code.

There are numerous prototyping tools available online. Here are just a few you can pick from:

- Fluid UI (http://fluidui.com): Fluid UI lets you quickly mock up your app without worrying about code. Figure 2-1 shows an example mockup for Android.

Figure 2-1. *An example user interface mockup made using Fluid UI*

- *Android GUI Prototyping* (http://www.artfulbits.com/products/free): If you're a Microsoft Visio user, you might want to consider using this stencil. You will need Visio 2003 or higher.

- *DroidDraw* (http://www.droiddraw.org/): A web-based designer/editor/builder for cell phone and tablet application programming on the Android platform. Currently in beta, it even generates the XML file that corresponds to the UI you've built. This is a big time-saver after you start writing code.

- *Pencil* (http://pencil.evolus.vn/en-US/Home.aspx): Designed by the Pencil Project, it is a free and open-source tool that can be used for graphical user interface (GUI) prototyping. Pencil includes a stencil for Android mockups. It comes as an application program that is available for Windows, Macintosh, and Linux. It is also available as a Firefox extension.

- *Fireworks Template for Android* (http://unitid.nl/2009/11/fireworks-template-for-android/): If you are an Adobe Fireworks user, you should consider this template, which has the Android user interface elements redrawn as vector images.

- *Android Wireframe Templates* (http://gliderguns.files.wordpress.com/2010/01/android_wireframe_templates3.pdf): If you're just at the ideation stage and want to play around with the overall idea, you can always use a paper and pencil to get started. These wireframe templates help you produce a more realistic layout. Actual Android phone illustrations are included for the HTC Dream, HTC Hero, HTC Magic, HTC Tattoo, HTC Nexus One, and Motorola Droid.

You may be considering creating an interface that is completely original. For example, you can go really crazy and do something like a funky style of pop-up book; or something that is more than just the usual bundle of buttons, pull-up menus, and finger swipes. You should be aware that the UI for Android has a certain paradigm that, if violated, could break the user's mental model and therefore cause frustration. You need to have an excellent justification for violating standard design rules. Proceed with caution.

Tools for Setting up a Web Site

To test your market demand hypothesis, you will need to set up a web site so that you have a place to host your screen shots and app description. After all, you can't place a fake app in a real app marketplace!

Because entire books have been written about web site construction, we won't go into great detail about how to create a cool site. Just be sure that it looks professional. If your site looks too amateurish, you won't get a good read on the market demand. We've all visited sites that have made a bad impression, and that impression affects our buying decisions. If you are new to web site development, you may wish to use a service such as Weebly (see Figure 2-2) to set up your site.

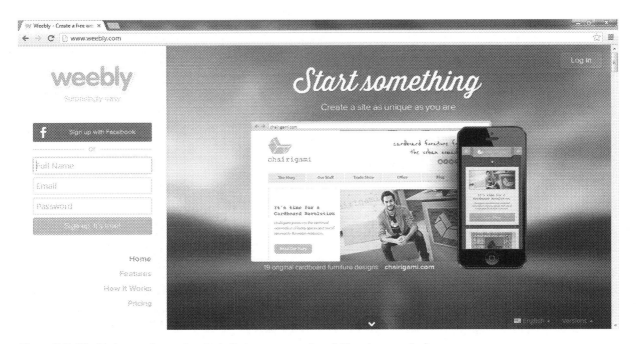

Figure 2-2. Weebly is one of many free tools that you can use to quickly set up a web site

Although your web site must look professional, it doesn't have to be highly developed. A few pages, possibly even one page, are all you need. Just make sure that your site matches the nature of your application. Here is where you can choose to include your icon, logo, screen shots, and any other stylistic aspects of your application. You might want to go to Google Play and select any application. Under each application should be a link to the developer's web site, so you can see what they look like. For example, Figure 2-3 shows the web site for the Waze app. The web page conveys the essence of the app. Waze is an extremely well known app, but you'll notice that the landing page is actually quite simple. It won't take very long to mock up your app's web site to the same level of completion.

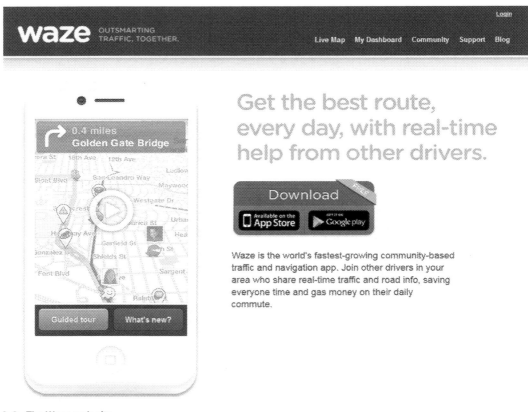

Figure 2-3. The Waze web site

There are numerous tools you can use to quickly build a web site. For the purposes of creating a quick site to test your business plan, we discuss only free online web-building software that hosts your page for free. These tools allow you to design your web site for free and they don't cost you a penny. Also, we selected tools that don't fill your web site with unprofessional-looking ads. Unfortunately, they all include a small footer at the bottom of the page, but they're not very distracting.

■ **Weebly** (www.weebly.com): Roy has had good results with Weebly (shown in Figure 2-2), which he has used to host his own web site. Weebly is very easy to use and offers a large selection of templates to choose from.

- **SnapPages** (`www.snappages.com`): This site builder is simple and hassle-free, and includes a number of web site templates.

- **Webnode** (`www.webnode.com`): This one is free for personal web sites and has hundreds of templates to choose from. You could always use a personal site to host your market demand hypothesis, and its paid service starts at $4.95/month.

Your Baby Might Be Ugly

It always hurts when people are quick to criticize something that took so long for you to put together. Like parents who have an ugly baby, developers often love their app in spite of a critical world. It's important to remember that even though you have given birth to a new idea, an app *isn't* a baby. A good entrepreneur can accept criticism. Sometimes, the facts just aren't in your favor, and your time is best spent looking for a new idea.

You're the Boss

We hope that this chapter has given you the tools you need to decide whether your idea has what it takes. The seven points listed earlier should drive you to ask tough questions about your Android application, and we stated some rules about what does and doesn't succeed in the world of Android applications. These are good rules to consider, but don't obsess over them; in reality, they're only guidelines. In other words, rules can be broken, but you break them at your own risk. We tried to spell out what rules to follow, but this is your journey to make.

Summary

Now that you know what's up, let's go through a little checklist:

- What problem are you solving?

- Is it a pain-killer or a vitamin?

- Who is your competition? What do you have that they don't?

- Who is the target market?

- How will you reach out to the target market?

- How long will it take to develop this app? Can you break the tasks into milestones?

- What technical risks must you solve? How can you prove to yourself they can be solved?

- Do you have the time and money to make this happen? Should you have a consultant evaluate your idea?

- Is the market large enough to provide your needed revenue stream?

- Is the market small enough that you can target its needs accurately?

- Is your target customer willing to pay?

- What Android version are you targeting?

- What pricing model are you using?

- Have you tested your market hypothesis?

- Do you want to stop answering questions and just break the rules? That's up to you, but proceed at your own risk.

Chapter 3

Legal Issues: Better Safe than Sorry

Roy has been involved in a number of legal actions, and he can tell you that they're never fun. A basic understanding of how the law impacts you as an app developer can keep you out of trouble. We aren't lawyers, and so we can't legally give you any specific legal advice. That said, maybe we can recommend some legal resources that you might find useful to avoid unnecessary unpleasantries.

Retaining an Attorney – Controlling Costs

You may be hesitant to involve an attorney because of the cost. Although attorneys are rarely inexpensive, they often cost a lot less than the consequences leveled against you. If you have any doubt about the legality of your app, or if you have any uncertainty about legal matters, you should get in touch with a lawyer immediately. Big name firms are great at what they do, but they are also very expensive. If you are working with limited means, you should consider going to a smaller law firm or perhaps to a single attorney working on his or her own. Often their rates will be more reasonable than at the big firms. Although they may not have the depth of expertise that a big firm does, they generally will do just fine at providing basic legal services. Ideally, you can find an attorney who has previously worked at a big firm and now has struck out on their own. They will have the experience of working at a big firm, but will charge more reasonable rates.

Remember that it is possible to negotiate rates with attorneys. If you meet with more than one firm, you will have more leverage to negotiate. For run-of-the-mill work (such as incorporating your company or writing generic employment contracts), it is often possible to request a fixed fee. You can then shop around between firms to make an apples-to-apples comparison of pricing.

Young lawyers, known as "junior associates" are generally only a few years out of law school and usually require on-the-job training. Be careful that you aren't paying to train an attorney. You can request the law firm not to use junior associates on your account. Typically, you will either want to have a partner at the firm do your work, or work with a senior associate. Only work with junior associates who have already done the type of work you are looking to have done. A typical arrangement is for the junior associate to do most of the work, which is then reviewed by a partner at the firm. Naturally, if a junior associate isn't doing things correctly, you're paying for the partner to fix his errors. You should be careful that you aren't paying for lawyers to meet with each other. In general, the fewer lawyers you involve, the more efficient the process will be.

If you are developing your app with a mindset to raise money from investors, you can sometimes convince attorneys to provide consulting without upfront costs, in an arrangement known as "deferred compensation." This typically results in some number of billable hours that are not charged until your company reaches a financing threshold agreed upon by you and the attorney. The attorney may also negotiate for some equity in your venture. Once you reach the financing threshold (often your first round of funding), you will be required to pay your outstanding balance. This sort of deal is generally offered only by firms who specialize in helping startups. This field is known in the industry as "Venture Capital Law." Often venture capital law firms will waive compensation if your company is unsuccessful in meeting its funding goals and is forced to dissolve. The specific terms often depend on your ability to sell yourself and your idea to the attorney. Remember, this payment structure is contingent on the idea that you are looking to raise enough money to more than cover your legal expenses. A venture capital law firm may offer you $10,000 to as high as $25,000 or more, in deferred consulting services. Remember, deferred doesn't mean free; you should be careful you aren't being overcharged for services. Unscrupulous attorneys may charge you more for the equivalent service because they know you will not be as attentive to costs with this billing structure.

The process of raising money from outside investors is a topic beyond the scope of this book, but remember that if you pursue that option you will be diluting your ownership in the company and using a lot of your time to fund-raise instead of building out your idea. If you believe the market is big enough, it can be a good choice, but there are pros and cons to consider.

Remember that you want to be careful about what terms you accept when you engage a lawyer. If you go to Best Law Firms, a web site from *US News and World Report* (http://bestlawfirms.usnews.com/) you will see a search engine that will help you find a law firm in your location for practice areas such as "Venture Capital Law" or "Corporate Law."

Forming Your Company

If you release an Android application under your own name, the law considers the business to be a sole proprietorship. You can certainly call your business whatever you want, but as a sole proprietorship, you are personally liable for any debt, wrongdoing, and/or negligence. For example, if you order supplies and can't pay them back because revenue is less than you projected, then you are personally liable for the debt. If your mapping app causes someone to drive off a cliff, they could, in principle, sue you personally for injuries. On the other hand, when the app is owned by a corporation (including LLCs, or limited liability corporations), liability generally attaches to the separate legal entity. To explain this in a bit more detail, the formation of the legal entity separates the assets and liabilities of the business from the assets and liabilities of the owner or owners. Therefore, it is often desirable to form a corporate entity to shield yourself against lawsuits and debts attributable to the app you have written. There are also some potential tax advantages to forming a corporation; you will be able to write off certain business expenses, which could save you money in the long term.

Remember that you have to be careful to honor the separation of assets and liabilities, or the courts may not shield you from personal liability. For example, if you use the company's funds for personal matters, that would clearly violate the idea that your personal assets and corporate assets are separate. It's also illegal and could result in charges of embezzlement from your creditors or shareholders.

There are different types of corporate entities you can pick from. C Corporations, S Corporations, and Limited Liability Companies (LLCs) all have their own unique advantages and tax implications. There are many books on this subject written by legal experts, and because we are not lawyers, we refer you to them for more details.

EULA and Privacy Policies

A EULA is an "End-User License Agreement." Most often, a EULA presents your users with fancy legalese that they must agree to in order to access a web site or install a software package.

In essence, a EULA is a contract between you and your users. It establishes the terms and conditions under which an end user may use your app. A EULA provides a way to protect yourself from lawsuits in the event that the software causes damage to the user's computer or data, or by users who use your app in ways you never intended. For example, if your app is used to prepare taxes, you could use a EULA to limit damages when users use your software incorrectly and are subsequently penalized by the IRS. And by the way, if that's your app idea, we urge you to talk to a lawyer before going any further.

There are many complex legal issues governing the legal enforceability of EULAs, so if you feel your app needs one, again we urge you to contact an attorney with experience drafting contracts of this type. Many Android apps go without EULAs, and often it is the larger app companies (which can afford lawyers) that include them. However, each situation is unique, and you should think deeply about whether you are willing to go without the legal protections that a EULA affords you.

Examples of EULAs can often be found online. There are an infinite variety of EULAs, and it wouldn't be possible for us to recommend one to suit your particular needs. As always, we urge you to speak with an attorney if you have questions regarding this topic.

If you elect to include a EULA, you will want a way to programmatically display it in your app. Sample code to do just that can be found here:

```
http://blog.donnfelker.com/2011/02/17/android-a-simple-eula-for-your-android-apps/
```

A number of jurisdictions worldwide consider the right to privacy to be a legally protected concept. In particular, Europe has highly developed laws in this area. Although the United States has no federally mandated privacy policy requirements, both California and Connecticut require privacy policies for web sites and online services. As a result, to ensure that your app is legal in all jurisdictions in which it may be used, you should include and follow a privacy policy. In general, you need to be up front with the users as to what data you collect, and properly secure any personal information such as credit card numbers, driver's license numbers, and so forth.

The Mobile Marketing Association (a global nonprofit trade association) provides a free Mobile Application Privacy Policy that you can use. The policy is short at six pages, and all you need to do is fill in the blanks regarding your app's specifics. You can get the policy from the following link:

```
http://www.mmaglobal.com/node/18771?filename=MMA_Mobile_Application_Privacy_Policy_15Dec2011PC_
Update_FINAL.pdf
```

The Google Play Marketplace considers privacy of vital importance, so in addition to showing the user what your app will access (location, contacts, etc.) it also provides an optional link to your privacy policy. You can also host a web site that includes your privacy policy.

Although the privacy policy is currently optional, an agreement made by Google and five other major tech sector companies with the California Attorney General makes it likely that they will become mandatory sometime in the near future. It should go without saying that you must comply with the stated terms of your privacy policy. If you don't, you could be prosecuted under a number of laws, including California's Unfair Competition Law and/or False Advertising Law granting "the right of the public to protection from fraud and deceit."

Intellectual Property

You're planning to make money by distributing something that's really just a bunch of programs and data sitting in memory. Fortunately, even though software isn't a physical object, you can still protect it from theft just like real property. On the flip side, you can also be accused of stealing intellectual property. We think you'll agree that a little background on the laws of intellectual property is something every developer should have. Let's focus on four different flavors of intellectual property: copyrights, trademarks, trade secrets, and patents.

Copyrights

A copyright gives a creator of an original work (such as a book, photograph, or software) an exclusive right to it for a limited time. Specifically, a copyright holder is granted the right to dictate who can copy, distribute, publicly perform, modify, or create derivative works from their original work of authorship. This means that as the creator of an app, you alone have the right to copy, sell, or transmit the app for the duration of the copyright. Of course, you can assign that right to others if you choose. In most jurisdictions, a copyright lasts at least 50 years after the author's death. It's often longer than that.

For these reasons, you might be interested in obtaining a copyright. The good news is that it's very easy to get. In legal terms, the moment that you put your pen to the paper or type characters into the computer, copyright protection is granted. Copyright can protect aspects such as source code, graphics, sound effects, and other original creative works you put in your application, but it does not protect any facts or ideas that are not used in a creative or artistic way. To protect an invention, you should get a patent, as discussed in the "Patents" section later in this chapter.

Obtaining a copyright can give you a base level of protection that would come in handy when suing an obvious imitator of your work The emphasis in that last sentence is *obvious* because copyright protection can extend for cases when your competitor is stealing graphics or the application itself, but not be applied when an imitator's application is coincidentally the same basic idea as yours.

Registering your copyright isn't required in order to benefit from copyright protection. However, copyright registration is *prima facie* evidence of a valid copyright. Registration enables the copyright holder to seek statutory damages and attorney's fees if filed within 3 months of publication or before there is an infringement. Otherwise, the owner can sue only for actual damages and profits.

Registration, which can be done online, requires that you upload the first 25 and last 25 pages of your source code (preferably in PDF format). It is up to you to decide what the first and last pages of your application are. Every new version of your application must be re-registered. You can also register screen shots of your application. Detailed instructions can be found here:

http://www.copyright.gov/circs/circ61.pdf

Although not required to enjoy copyright protections, including a copyright notice (whether in words or with the copyright symbol) can help to overcome a presumption of "innocent infringement." In other words, if the copyright violator saw that your work was copyrighted, the act of copying it couldn't have been innocent.

The current filing fee is $65, but it is only $35 if filed online at `http://www.copyright.gov/eco/`. You can find answers to a lot of your electronic filing questions at the tutorial available at `http://www.copyright.gov/eco/eco-tutorial.pdf`.

Trademarks

Now let's talk about trademarks. Trademarks are intended to keep others from confusing your company's products and services with someone else's. A trademark does not protect the concept or idea, but it will protect you from others operating under your name and logo, or its likeness. In today's market, protecting your brand is extremely important. Think about companies such as McDonald's, Microsoft, and, for the sake of argument, Google's very own Android. No doubt images of their logos come to mind: the golden arches, the Windows symbol, and that green robot guy, respectively. Trademark law keeps competitors from using those logos in a way that could confuse consumers.

Trademark rights are not granted automatically, unlike copyrights. However, you may be able to pursue legal action for an unlicensed trademark under a common law principle called "passing off." The moment you use a name or symbol as an identifier for your Android application, you may have access to protection under that law. However, the law requires that you establish that there is "goodwill" owned by the trader, namely you. That will be difficult to do unless you have a bunch of customers that know you by your mark. Within the United States, you might want to secure better protection by filing a trademark registration with the U.S. Patent and Trademark Office, which is needed to pursue a trademark action in federal court. Once your trademark is granted, you get protection without having to prove that your mark is well known. Outside of the United States, you will find that most countries offer similar trademark protections as dictated by the World Trade Organization's TRIPS (Trade Related Aspects of Intellectual Property Rights) agreement. It can be expensive to pursue trademark protection on a worldwide basis, so you should think about where you will most benefit from these protections and then limit your applications to those regions.

Among other issues, if someone else is already using the trademark you are planning to use, you may not receive any protection, and may even be infringing on their trademark. The U.S. Patent and Trademark Office maintains a database of registered trademarks. You can search this database using the Trademark Electronic Search System (TESS) for free, but you should employ a trademark attorney to help you interpret the results and register your trademark. You can access the trademark process and search details here:

`http://www.uspto.gov/trademarks/`

Protecting Your Trade Secrets

When developing your intellectual property, there are some things that you probably wouldn't divulge to the average person. As a professional blogger, Mark doesn't state his business contacts on his individual blog posts, and there are strategies that he doesn't share with everyone. These sorts of things are protected by trade secret law.

In particular under U.S. law, "A trade secret, as defined under 18 U.S.C. § 1839(3) (A), (B) (1996), has three parts: (1) information; (2) reasonable measures taken to protect the information; and (3) which derives independent economic value from not being publicly known." Trade secrets do not have a limited lifetime like a copyright, trademark, or patent. However, a third party that discovers your secret independently is not in violation of its provisions.

As you can see, if you expect to benefit from the protections of trade secret law, you have to take reasonable measures to protect the information in question. For example, you will want to password protect your critical data and shred any documents that contain sensitive information. If you have people working for you or with you on your Android application, then they need to know the importance of keeping all application-related information on private drives and servers, and it is important to require them to sign a confidentiality contract such as non-disclosure agreement (NDA).

There are numerous sample NDAs available online. You can use them to get started, but as with all legal matters, you should always consult an attorney to resolve any legal questions specific to your situation.

Here are some samples you can look over:

```
http://www.hbs.edu/entrepreneurship/pdf/Sample_NDA.pdf
```

```
http://www.bitlaw.com/forms/nda.html
```

If your trade secrets are stolen, and you can prove to a court that you made reasonable efforts to keep your trade secrets confidential, then you are potentially entitled to different legal remedies, including injunctions and an award of damages.

Patents

Now that we have discussed the laws of copyright, patents, and trademarks, let's get into patents. A patent is a written public disclosure of an invention. In return for making a public disclosure (which, in theory, enriches the world with new knowledge) an inventor is granted the right to stop other people from making, using, selling, offering for sale, or importing the subject of the invention for a period of time. Most Android developers are not likely to benefit from filing for their own patents because obtaining one is an extremely costly venture. Suing another company for infringement is even more costly; a patent lawsuit can easily run into seven figures. The average patent can easily cost $10,000 or more over its lifetime. Furthermore, few Android apps will qualify for a patent.

If you decide to pursue a patent, be aware that not any idea can qualify for one. Any "new and useful process, machine, manufacture, or composition of matter, or any new and useful improvement thereof" may be patented, but the subject of the invention must also be novel and non-obvious. A patent examiner will determine whether your invention meets the requirement of being both novel (new) and non-obvious by comparing your invention with existing inventions, known as prior art. Obviously, if your idea has already been invented, you should not expect to receive a patent for it. Additionally, any similar inventions that taken alone or together would render your invention obvious also preclude patentability. A good patent attorney (or a bad patent examiner!) can make it easier for your patent to pass muster.

You will want to search to see whether your app idea already exists (is there prior art?) before proceeding with your app. If it exists, but is not patented, then you will not be able to get a patent. If it exists and *is* patented, then you will be infringing on the patent owner's rights if you attempt to make the app yourself. As always, we recommend you contact an attorney; in this case, a patent attorney. However, a simple Google search is a great way to search for prior art on your own. Additionally, Google can search specifically for patents by using this link:

```
http://www.google.com/?tbm=pts
```

Let's say you're certain your app meets the requirements for novelty and non-obviousness. You're also certain it will earn you much more than the $10,000+ plus it will cost to file for a patent. One way to hedge your bet is the provisional patent application. This is a legal process that allows you to send a basic description of your invention to the patent office, and use that description to establish a patent filing date for your invention. This process costs only $130 for a small entity, but changes annually. You have a nonextendable 1-year deadline to file a regular patent application at the normal fee. The advantage of the provisional patent is that it allows you to claim your invention for a low cost, and then you have a year to decide if it's worth your trouble to spend "real money" in order to secure your patent rights. The provisional patent also gives you the right to use the "patent pending" term that you see attached to many product ads. In case you are wondering what it means, it simply states to competitors that there is a patent application in the works on your product and/or service. You can file for a provisional patent application online through this web site:
```
https://efs.uspto.gov/efile/portal/efs-unregistered.
```

Licensing

It is tempting to leverage open-source software when writing your app. There are a great many free software libraries that do all sorts of amazing things. Most of them, however, are licensed under a variety of open-source licenses. Failure to comply with the terms of these licenses could leave you open to legal action. As an example, the Creative Commons license expressly forbids any commercial use. The General Public License (GPL) raises a number of legal ambiguities regarding linking your non-GPL software with GPL libraries. Some people believe that although statically linking with a GPL library is a violation of the license, dynamically linking is OK. In contrast, the LPGL (Lesser General Public License) categorically allows linking with non-LGPL software. The following were just a few examples of licensing terms. In short, you should research the license for a piece of free software before using it.

Many patented inventions can also be licensed. In the world of software, examples of technologies that require licenses include MPEG, MP3, and Dolby Digital. In many cases, the phone (or tablet) manufacturer has already negotiated for these sorts of licenses, but if you find yourself using a standard that isn't already included with the Android SDK, you may want to double-check to avoid any trouble. You can find a list of commonly licensed standards in this link:

```
http://www.musemagic.com/papers/licensinginfo.html
```

Also, if you discover someone else has patented the exact idea you're looking to implement as an app, then it might be worth it to contact them before giving up. Often inventors are interested in licensing their ideas, and are hoping someone contacts them with that in mind.

Summary

Although you might not want to worry about legal issues and just get down to the nuts and bolts of writing, marketing, and selling software, it pays to invest a little time up front to avoid big problems in the future. You may have noticed that some of the topics we discussed make more sense if your app is backed by some outside funding. In particular, incorporating as a C Corp, finding a venture capital law firm, and considering pursuing patents are often better suited to well-funded ventures. However, even a modest venture should at least spend some time finding a local attorney who can help with company formation. Even if you think it makes sense to go forward as a sole proprietorship, you can often have a short discussion with an attorney for free just to make sure. Spending a bit of time thinking about whether you app needs a EULA or privacy policy is also a good idea for even a modest venture. Of course, if you think you might be infringing someone else's intellectual property rights, you have a big problem right from the get-go. In short, do a little homework at the beginning, and you'll be able to approach the rest of your business planning with confidence!

The following is a checklist of potential legal issues. Remember, we recommend you consult with an attorney before making any business decisions.

- Have you incorporated or otherwise mitigated risk of personal liability?

- Have you begun thinking about your EULA and/or privacy policy?

- Are you infringing anyone else's copyrights, trademarks, or patents? If so, can you get a license?

- Are you following good privacy practices, including requiring your developers and partners to sign NDAs, and devising a plan to secure all personal information?

Chapter 4

A Brief Introduction to Android Development

By now, you have seen that there is a method to the madness of marketing Android apps. Chapter 2 discussed coming up with that million-dollar idea, and Chapter 3 covered some legal technicalities. This chapter takes you through the first steps of actually creating an Android application.

If you are an experienced programmer, you might find the information in this chapter too basic, so it might seem more of a review. If so, by all means scan it quickly and move on to subsequent chapters that focus on marketing Android applications.

If you are a first-time developer, you should read this chapter very carefully to understand the concepts involved. We wrote this book so that anyone can succeed in the current Android market, so it helps to learn as much as possible before you write that first line of code for your application.

If you are just beginning to write an application for Android, you might discover a lot of technical terms being thrown around, and it might be difficult to navigate this sea of abbreviations. Although we can't teach you to write Android applications in one chapter, we can give you a very high-level overview that we hope will give you the guidance you need for learning more on your own.

First Steps as a Developer

If you are just starting out as an Android developer, you need the Android Developer Tools (ADT) bundle. You also need the Java Development Kit (JDK) to use the ADT because the Eclipse integrated development environment (IDE) is written in Java. If you do not have the JDK installed on your computer, you should install it before you install the ADT. You can download the JDK from the Oracle web site: `http://www.oracle.com/technetwork/java/javase/downloads/index.html`

After you install the standard Java JDK, you can install the Android ADT bundle from the Android software development kit (SDK) web site. This bundle includes nearly everything you need to get started with the SDK and the Eclipse IDE. It also includes other development tools, such as an emulator you can use to simulate an Android device for testing. The ADT also includes documentation for the Android application programming interface (API), source code for the Android platform, and samples demonstrating how to use a number of the API elements. With one click, you can download everything you need: `http://developer.android.com/sdk/index.html`

The ADT bundle supports Windows (with 32-bit and 64-bit options), but other bundles also exist for Ubuntu Linux (8.04 or later) and Mac OS X (10.5.8 or later). The correct bundle for your operating system (OS) should appear as the default.

After you install the ADT bundle, we recommend that you surf over to Android's online developer resources. The best way to get information about Android is from the horse's mouth: `http://developer.android.com/index.html`

Take your time and look around. Everything you need to know about Android design, development, and distribution is available on the site. If you get confused, head back to this chapter. Our goal is to give you some basic orientation, but the materials available online are more extensive.

If you want information specific to Android applications, the following link is also very helpful: `http://developer.android.com/guide/components/fundamentals.html`

After you install the Android ADT bundle, you can review a great introduction to app development: `http://developer.android.com/training/index.html`

Integrated Development Environment (IDE)

Authors tend to write by using a word processor; developers tend to code with an IDE. An IDE is an application, somewhat similar to a word processor, that enables you to see and modify source code. Source code is typically color-coded in a way that highlights keywords and syntax. In addition, an IDE checks the syntax (structure) of your code as you write and is integrated (hence the name) with development tools such as compilers and debuggers. IDEs have lots of very useful capabilities that make writing software easier and more enjoyable.

Eclipse is a well-known, open-source IDE that is mostly written in Java and built around the idea of plug-ins. Eclipse has plug-ins for almost everything, including development, debugging, and revision control in many different programming languages. Although not directly related to Android development (just as knowing how to use a word processor isn't directly related to writing), it is very powerful and worth understanding. You can learn more here: `http://help.eclipse.org`

Android provides an Eclipse plug-in that is perfect for developing Android apps. The ADT plug-in customizes your Eclipse workspace for use with Android. It includes a guided project setup, custom editors for Android configuration files, debug output, and more. It does everything you need, right down to creating a release package that gets uploaded to Google Play and other marketplaces.

Alternatively, you can use commercial IDEs such as JetBrains' IntelliJ IDEA. IntelliJ comes in a free, open-source community edition and a commercial Ultimate Edition. Some developers swear by the Ultimate Edition, arguing that it has superior code indexing that results in better code completion, refactoring, and navigation. IntelliJ also supports plug-ins; that makes it a good candidate for Android development. You can learn more about using IntelliJ IDEA for Android Development here: `http://www.jetbrains.com/idea/features/android.html`

Perks of the Android Operating System

As discussed in Chapter 1, Android is a Linux-based OS that relies on Java to simplify software development. It makes heavy use of Extensible Markup Language (XML) to simplify coding tasks even more.

Android is based on the Linux open-source OS kernel. Because Linux is written in the C and Assembly programming languages, you can develop parts of your application using the OS's "native" language. The Android Native Development Kit (NDK) provides this capability to developers. Note that developing apps natively in C or C++ is not usually necessary and should be avoided unless a particular performance issue requires it. Among other issues, C/C++ development is specific to the underlying hardware, so your app is not guaranteed to be portable if you use C/C++ elements.

The software libraries that link the software in your application to the underlying hardware are collectively called application programming interfaces (APIs). Java APIs exist for interfacing with all the device hardware. A typical smartphone has quite a bit of hardware that needs to be supported. Of course, there are multitouch user interface capabilities such as swiping, tapping, and pinching. Internal hardware devices and sensors such as accelerometers (used to detect phone motion and rotation) are directly supported by the OS. Cameras, GPS, microphones, and virtually everything else a modern phone offers are accessible through Java APIs.

As a mobile OS, Android is designed from the ground up to minimize power consumption. This is reflected in the technique used to manage multiple applications. Applications not currently used are suspended—they wait in the background until they are needed again. This means that only the current application usually uses battery power. It also means that there is no reason to close apps. A user can simply start using the new app, and the suspended app waits around until it is needed again. If memory runs low, Android deletes the apps that are least likely to be missed by the user (the ones that have been used least). This way of managing applications is very different from how things work on a desktop OS. We go into more detail when we talk about the app life cycle later in this chapter.

In Android, new apps are typically installed through an online connection to the Google Play Store. New apps can be searched and perused via the Google Play application. If users choose to install a new app, they are informed about all the resources that the application needs access to. For example, it might need access to the user's phone book contacts or the phone's location. A user is therefore informed about the app's impact before the app is downloaded. Although not foolproof, this process provides some protection against malicious developers.

After an app is downloaded to the device, Android has a security model that further protects users from malicious applications. Each application runs in its own *sandbox*, which means that an application has limited access to system resources and is limited in its capability to harm the user, either through an accidental bug or via an intentionally malicious hack.

In practice, the security sandbox is implemented through a number of measures. Android is Linux at its heart, and Linux supports multiple users. Android extends this support to apps. Just as one user is limited in his or her ability to access other users' data, the same is true for apps in Android. In technical terms, each app runs in its own process. For apps written in Java, each app also runs in its own instance of the Dalvik virtual machine. We will explain more about Dalvik later in this chapter, but for now, you should know that it keeps apps from interacting with each other without specifically designed message passing. There are a number of other technical aspects to the security sandbox, but the key is that Android implements the principle of least privilege: an application gets access only to the system resources it requires—and no more.

Java the Language

Java is a logical choice for mobile app development. It is the second most popular computer language in the world, according to langpop.com, which means that many developers already know it, and a large infrastructure of software development resources already exists.

Android uses Java in the sense that code written for Android follows all Java syntax requirements. Android's version of Java is, however, significantly different from Oracle's standard version of Java, both in terms of how it is executed and its supported libraries. We discuss these differences in the next section, but let's first talk about factors that are common to all variants of Java.

Even if you do not know anything about Java, it is relatively easy for any programmer to pick up. Its syntax is similar to C, C++, C#, and Objective C. If you know any of these languages and understand the fundamentals of object-oriented programming (OOP), you start with a big advantage over other beginners.

Java is notable in that it executes within a virtual machine. Unlike traditionally compiled languages such as C or C++, the same Java binary (consisting of Java bytecode) can run on any hardware platform, as long as a Java virtual machine has been written for that platform. This makes Java code extremely portable.

Like many modern programming languages, Java is object-oriented. So as a developer, you are supposed to write your software as a collection of interacting objects, each of which solves a particular problem. The object-oriented paradigm encourages good coding practices and makes your software easily reusable. As you might expect, Android APIs actively support and promote this style of development.

Unlike C, C++, and Objective C, Java automatically manages the computer's memory for you in the background (with only a small performance penalty), so you do not have to remember to delete data structures that are no longer being used. In fact, Java does not require the programmer to manipulate pointers, which are common in many lower-level languages. For any developer who has struggled with pointers and memory leaks (including Roy), this is a welcome change that definitely reduces development and debugging times.

Another great Java feature is reflection: a program can look at its own software objects and modify them while it is running. It's sort of like operating on yourself, but painful only in that it can make your head spin. Reflection has many practical benefits to you as a developer. Many testing frameworks (such as JUnit, discussed in a later section) use reflection to provide a higher level of intelligence about the code being tested.

Another powerful example of the benefits of reflection is found in Eclipse. Using reflection, the Eclipse environment understands the code you write as you write it. So it can, for example, point out errors in your code in real time.

Java is full featured. An extensive set of APIs means that nearly every data structure or software framework you could ever want is readily available. In many cases, non–Android Java software packages can simply be dropped into your development environment as prepackaged builds known as Java Archive (JAR) files.

Although we could devote an entire book to learning Java, we won't because our publisher already sells them. Some good starting points are available in these books:

- *Learn Java for Android Development*, by Jeff Friesen (Apress, 2013)
- *Android Apps with Eclipse*, by Onur Cinar (Apress, 2012)
- *Android Recipes: A Problem-Solution Approach*, by Dave Smith and Jeff Friesen (Apress, 2012)

Many free online resources are available and just a few mouse clicks away, including `http://www.oracle.com/technetwork/java/index-jsp-135888.html` and `http://mobile.tutsplus.com/tutorials/android/java-tutorial/`.

Peculiarities of Java on Android

Android is known for using its own virtual machine, Dalvik. Traditionally, Java has used the Java Virtual Machine (JVM), which executes .class files. Dalvik converts .class files into a Dalvik Executable (DEX) file. Dalvik is optimized for low-memory requirements and differs from a conventional JVM (such as the one supported by Oracle) in numerous ways. Fortunately, these differences are largely invisible to developers because of the Android build tools that automatically converts non–Android class files into a Dalvik-compatible executable.

Unfortunately, there are practical differences that those familiar with traditional Java will encounter. Android uses its own graphical user interface (GUI) library. Java Standard Edition (SE) provides the Swing GUI, the primary Java GUI widget toolkit that is completely unsupported on Android. Any Swing code has to be completely rewritten. But the Android GUI does have practical benefits. By relying heavily on XML definitions, Android simplifies GUI design and promotes more human-readable interfaces.

Android makes heavy use of XML, which is simply a text format that is designed to be understood by both humans and machines. As a developer, any time you convey standard information to the OS in a text file, you use XML. Besides their use in GUI design, XML files can store text strings used by your app. Although you can get by without storing text strings in XML the advantages are worth the trouble.

A well-written Android app stores its strings in XML files located in the /res/values directory. The XML format includes identifiers that let the OS know that string text data is contained in the file. Any time you need access to a string in your application, you can refer to it in your code using the identifier R.string.*string_name.* Not only does this improve the readability of your code but it also allows Android utilities to automatically internationalize your application.

Before you release your app, Android utilities exist to automatically translate your /res/values/strings.xml file. It will be automatically translated into different languages so that users around the world can use your app in their native tongue. Granted, the translations won't be perfect, so in most cases you'll need to have someone look over each translation and clean up any issues. Also, you'll need to copy the translated files into a series of directories for each language you plan to support. For example, the French translation could live in a directory called values-fr. Still, not bad for a little extra effort, huh? You can learn more about automatic translation here: `http://googledevelopers.blogspot.com/2012/03/localize-your-apps-and-content-more.html`

We mentioned that the string XML files are stored in the /res/values directory. The *res* stands for *resources*, a very powerful concept in Android. Android makes heavy use of resource files and tightly integrates them with Java. You just saw how resource file strings can be accessed in your code. Similarly, drawable resources such as icons and images can also be accessed programmatically through Java. The XML files used for GUI layout are also resources. Finally, arbitrary files such as sound samples can be accessed as resources.

There are numerous other differences between the Android API and the one used by traditional Java. Notably, the following packages, normally a part of the Java 2 Platform Standard Edition, are missing:

- `java.applet`
- `java.awt`
- `java.beans`
- `java.lang.management`
- `java.rmi`
- `javax.accessibility`
- `javax.activity`
- `javax.imageio`
- `javax.management`
- `javax.naming`
- `javax.print`
- `javax.rmi`
- `javax.security.auth.kerberos`
- `javax.security.auth.spi`
- `javax.security.sasl`
- `javax.swing`
- `javax.transaction`
- `javax.xml` (except `javax.xml.parsers`)
- `org.ietf.*`
- `org.omg.*`
- `org.w3c.dom.*` (subpackages)

Additionally, the following third-party packages are included:

- `org.apache.commons.codec`: Utilities for encoding and decoding
- `org.apache.commons.httpclient`: HTTP authentication, cookies, methods, and protocol
- `org.bluez`: Bluetooth support
- `org.json`: JavaScript Object Notation (JSON)

A detailed description of the entire Android API can be found on Google's `developer.android.com` web site: `http://developer.android.com/reference/android/package-summary.html`

The App Life Cycle

The single biggest difference you will encounter when coming from a traditional Java programming background is the Android application life cycle. If you have a background in developing applications for personal computers, the Android application life cycle will be a revelation.

Before Android can even download an application from Google Play, it gathers some information about it. That information is stored in an XML file called AndroidManifest.xml. This file *must* be in your application's root directory. The manifest includes information about the package and name of your application, its components, the permissions your application needs, the minimum-level Android API that the application requires to run, and the software libraries your application needs to access.

Google Play uses this information to determine whether it can even show an application to an end user. For example, if your phone doesn't support an app's required minimum API level, you won't see the app if you search for it.

If you can download the app, the manifest also dictates how the app is run. An application consists of four basic building blocks called application components. Possible components are Activities, Services, Content Providers, and Broadcast Receivers.

Here's a very brief summary of these building blocks:

- An Activity is a piece of code that outputs a single screen. If your app has a phone book and a configuration page, they are separate Activities.

- A Service provides a background task to your application. For example, if your application needs to listen for data even when your application isn't active, you need to use a Service.

- A Content Provider allows your application to share its data with other applications. It isn't likely to be necessary for a basic app.

- A Broadcast Receiver lets your application listen to announcements from the OS or other applications. For example, if your application needs to know that the screen has changed from portrait to landscape mode, you can use a Broadcast Receiver.

The manifest includes references to all the application components for your application. Using the manifest, the OS can also determine which application Activity component is the one it should run when you launch the application.

Let's assume that you started your app, and the OS has determined that an Activity called "phone book" is the one that it should initially launch. Each Activity follows an activity life cycle that supports Android's power-saving, always-available application model.

Even the most bare-boned Android application conforms to an Activity life cycle that governs the life of the application. Again, an Android application is not supposed to be designed to exit. The OS decides when apps are forced into the background and when they are stopped.

Consequently, unlike traditional application development, your application does not have a "quit" or "exit" option. Instead, you must write code that supports certain OS hooks. These hooks are different for each application component, but the Activity component is the most commonly used and perhaps the most complicated.

Here are the essential stages in the Activity life cycle, also illustrated in Figure 4-1.

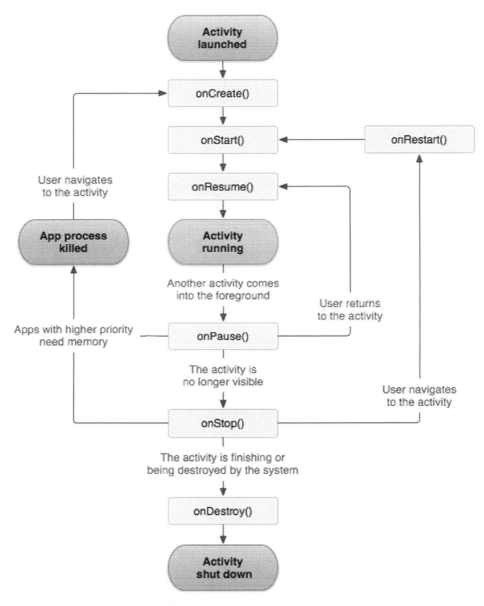

Figure 4-1. *The important state paths of an Activity[1]*

---

[1]Figure 4-1 is reproduced from work created and shared by the Android Open Source Project and used according to terms described in the Creative Commons 2.5 Attribution License. http://developer.android.com/reference/android/app/Activity.html#ActivityLifecycle

▓ **onCreate**: Called when an Activity is first created. The Activity might start and stop after it is created, but this stage addresses an Activity that isn't presently in memory and must be initialized.

▓ **onStart**: Called immediately after onCreate and also immediately after onRestart (see the onRestart bullet that follows). It is also called any time the application becomes visible to the user.

▓ **onResume**: Called after onStart when the Activity is capable of accepting user input.

▓ **onStop:** Called when the Activity is no longer visible because another Activity has replaced it in the foreground. The OS might now choose to delete the memory currently being used by the application to reclaim system memory. If this occurs, the application must be rerun using onCreate if it is called again.

▓ **onRestart:** Called after onStop when the Activity resumes.

▓ **onPause:** Called when the present Activity is being replaced with another Activity. This is where you save state information, but it must be done quickly to avoid lag. Not only will you delay the upcoming application but if you wait too long, you could also trigger an Application Not Responding (ANR) error. Store your persistent data and move out of the way.

▓ **onDestroy:** Called when your Activity is complete. The OS might now choose to delete your application to conserve memory.

As you can see, this process can be quite complicated and confusing for the uninitiated. We recommend that you spend time studying the life cycle diagram and playing with example applications to get some grounding in this essential concept. Fortunately, all you will need are one or two Activity components for simple applications.

Notice that we have not discussed an actual "Application" component. That's because it doesn't exist. There is, however, an Application class object, but it's created automatically in the background. You have to worry about the Application class only if you need to track global information across multiple application components.

App Deployment

One of the main advantages of Android app development is the ease and flexibility with which an application can be deployed. If you are ready to deploy to a marketplace, Chapter 8 tells you everything you need to know.

But using marketplaces are only one way to distribute your applications. Particularly if your product is still in beta, you might want to release it through e-mail or from a protected page on your web site.

An Android app is automatically bundled as an Android Application Package (APK) file by the development environment. Android makes it absurdly easy to install APK files via e-mail. If you simply attach an APK file to an e-mail, recipients will see an Install button on their e-mail when they open it in Gmail with an Android-powered device. This trick works from the Gmail app (see Figure 4-2). When you access Gmail through a browser, there is no Install button, although the app can be downloaded and installed without any issues.

Figure 4-2. *An example of an APK file sent via Gmail*

Note that the recipient of the e-mail is free to forward the e-mail (and hence your app) to others. If your app is not intended for public disclosure, be sure to have recipients agree (in writing) to refrain from distributing your APK. Refer back to Chapter 2 for information about non-disclosure agreements.

An Android app is also incredibly easy to distribute from your web site. Simply include a link to an APK file on your site. When users click the link from an Android-powered device, the device prompts them to install the application. Of course, you could also place your app on DropBox, Google Drive, or any other file-sharing services. The Android OS understands that APK files are apps that can be installed and then acts accordingly.

Note, however, that Android protects users from malicious apps by preventing both e-mail and web-based distribution from unknown sources. Before users can install your app, they need to enable their devices to allow installation of apps from sources other than Google Play. This is simple; in the Settings app, they click either Applications or Security, and then check the option to allow Unknown Sources. Just be sure to explain this in the e-mail or on your web site. Naturally, it is safest if the user disables the Unknown Sources option after they finish.

This Is So Complicated! Is There an Easier Way?

Developing software is not a trivial exercise. Software developers earn a comfortable salary, and with good reason. This stuff isn't learned overnight. If you're not a programmer and you don't have the time to learn, however, there are a few alternatives. These options don't help for complicated apps, but if your app is simple, it might get you up and running faster.

MIT App Inventor is a drag-and-drop Android app development tool. It really is supported by MIT, and it's free. You can learn more here: `http://appinventor.mit.edu/`

Appnotch is another drag-and-drop service that allows you to develop apps for Android (and iOS). The basic version of Appnotch Lite is free, but it also has paid versions—Appnotch Elite, Pro, Team, and Enterprise: `http://www.appnotch.com/`

Appery.io is yet another service that allows you to develop apps for Android (and iOS and Windows Phone). The Starter version is free, but Appery.io also hosts Pro, Premium, and Enterprise versions: `http://appery.io`

There are numerous other online app builders. If you go this route, we recommend that you spend some time exploring online. This is a rapidly evolving area, and we can't recommend one particular solution as being the best.

Summary

If you want to learn to program with Android, here are some questions you should answer first:

- Have you set up the Android ADT?

- Do you understand the basics of Java programming?

- Have you followed the online tutorial provided by Android?

- Do you know the Android application life cycle?

- Should you learn Android app development or are you better off either outsourcing your work or using an app builder? If you're looking for an Android developer, Roy, one of the authors, is happy to lend a hand!

Chapter 5

Develop Apps Like a Pro

Chapter 4 provided a brief introduction to Android development. In a similar vein, we want to give you a brief overview of professional software development techniques. Whether you're learning to code or simply want to evaluate the skill set of a developer you are hiring, this chapter will give you enough background to start asking the right questions.

We will cover software engineering methodologies, debugging, revision control, issue tracking, unit testing, and system testing. If you are serious about software development, you should be familiar with all these topics. If you are interviewing developers, you can be sure they are inexperienced if they can't speak authoritatively about these subjects.

Software Engineering

Software projects are notorious for running over budget and schedule. An academic field called software engineering creates and investigates processes that can keep this from happening. Let's spend a moment discussing what processes are used.

In the traditional waterfall model of software development, there is a series of steps that are followed one after the other, like a multitiered waterfall.

The first step is requirements analysis, in which the requirements for the project are collected. One might detail the purpose of the software and try to define its interfaces without getting into coding issues. A lot of the principles discussed in Chapter 2 that relate to your business plan can be considered requirements analysis.

The second step is design, in which the interaction between software components is determined. Modern software design makes frequent use of "design patterns," which are established ways of architecting code. For example, Android makes heavy use of the Model-View-Controller (MVC) design pattern. If your Android user interface (UI) isn't consistent with MVC principles, you're probably not writing clean code. When it comes to the UI, you can design mockups using the software packages mentioned in the "User Interface" section of Chapter 2.

The third step is implementation, when the code is actually written. You need to understand the techniques and concepts discussed in Chapter 4 to do this.

The design must then be verified, which means tested. We will talk about how to do that later in this chapter. Finally, in an ongoing process, the code must be maintained over its useful lifetime.

The waterfall model is often criticized for being too rigid to accurately reflect the process of designing software. For example, it is typical for new features to be added after the design stage has been finished. New requirements often arise only after the code has been partially tested.

Agile software development, a more modern method, attempts to solve some of these problems. In Agile, software releases occur frequently, which introduces more checkpoints to test against customer requirements and more opportunities to add new customer requirements. Agile development focuses on creating a tight feedback loop between the customer and the developers (see Figure 5-1). There are many flavors of Agile software development, including Scrum and Extreme Programming (XP).

Figure 5-1. A model for developing software
Source: http://en.wikipedia.org/wiki/File:Agile_Software_Development_methodology.svg

There are many software engineering methodologies available, and we encourage you to read about them. To get started, we recommend the following book: *Being Agile: Your Roadmap to Successful Adoption of Agile* by Mario E. Moreira (Apress, 2013). At the time of writing, the book is in the alpha stage and is part of the Apress Alpha Program (see `http://www.apress.com/9781430258391`).

Documenting Your Code

Another pro development tip, and definitely not an optional one, is to document your code. Documentation is a critical step. Even if you're the only programmer, you will forget what your code does soon after you write it. Think about documentation as a way of writing notes to your future self. If you have more than one developer, or you plan to have more than one developer in the future, documentation is a must. Undocumented code is extremely difficult for a new programmer to learn.

Documenting code doesn't have to be difficult. With a few choice comments right in the code and some well-named variables, you'll be on your way. If you're new to Java, you should have a look at the Javadoc tool. By following its format with your comments, you can autogenerate beautiful HTML-formatted pages that fully document your code. Most Java API documentation is generated using Javadoc. You can learn more about Javadoc at `http://www.oracle.com/technetwork/java/javase/documentation/index-jsp-135444.html`.

Debugging Android Apps

When implementing and verifying code (refer to the waterfall model of software development in the preceding "Software Engineering" section), developers inevitably encounter errors. Anyone who has ever done any coding knows that more time is spent tracking bugs than actually writing code. Simple syntax errors are one thing; they are usually easy to find using a modern integrated development environment (IDE). The real challenges are the errors in which the code compiles just fine, but a little insidious problem keeps rearing its head. You try everything to track it down, but to no avail. If you want to develop your app like a pro, you should use the logging and debugging capabilities of Android.

The Logger

The logging facilities of Android are implemented in the Log class, which is built into the operating system. Using the logger is as simple as making a call like this:

```
Log.d(MY_APP, "Hello, world.");
```

If you're new to logging, the idea is that writing debug information out to a console is a basic way to debug the operation of your software. By reading the log messages your code outputs to the console, you can figure out what is happening when your code executes. You simply add calls to the logger wherever you want insight into what your code is doing. The Log object can be called in a number of ways. The `Log.d(...)` method sends a DEBUG log, the `Log.e(...)` method sends an ERROR log, the `Log.i(...)` method sends an information log, the `Log.v(...)` method sends a VERBOSE log, and the `Log.w(...)` method sends a warning log message.

These logging types can be used to represent different kinds of information. They also are assigned a priority. For example, ERROR logs are higher priority than DEBUG logs. You can think of the priorities as watermarks, and you configure your software for the watermark you need. If you are testing your software, you would probably want to see DEBUG logs as well as ERROR logs. But if your software is being released to customers, you might want to avoid the performance hit logging causes, and only log the ERROR messages.

Notice that the "Hello world" Log.d(...) example references MY_APP. MY_APP is a placeholder for a String class that you create. This string should be declared as follows in your app:

```
private static final String MY_APP = "MyActivity";
```

You can use any string you want, and you can later search for that string in the log output. You can even use multiple strings to represent different types of log data.

You can view log strings using the Dalvik Debug Monitor Server (DDMS) debugger that is built into the Android ADT version of Eclipse. Simply go to the DDMS Perspective in Eclipse, and you should see a LogCat window in which your Log message will appear. You can filter by text by creating a filter for that window.

The Debugger

As you might have guessed, the DDMS debugger does more than just list log messages. A debugger is used for exactly what it sounds like. A typical debugger enables you to step line by line through your code. You can also run your program and have it stop at a breakpoint that you set, and you can usually examine the state of internal variables. Finally, as we just explained, debuggers usually let you output log messages at particular points in your code. The Java DDMS debugger offers even more because of the reflection mechanisms inherent to the Java language.

The DDMS debugger IDE provides you with a list of currently running threads in your application and the current heap usage. It also enables you to track the memory allocated to different objects and allows you to explore the device's file system.

To learn more about debugging, see

```
http://developer.android.com/tools/debugging/debugging-projects.html.
```

Revision Control

When you have a particularly devious bug, you might make lots of little changes to the code to test out different hypotheses. Sometimes you end up making things worse, and you just wish you could get the code looking like it did originally. In other cases, you want to be able to compare differences between previous versions to see whether the differences could explain a bug that you're seeing. For these reasons, you should save each version of your program in a way that allows you to track changes and also go back and start fresh. This process is called *version control* or *revision control*.

Junior developers often think revision control is useful only for large shared projects, in which lots of developers are touching the same code base. But that overlooks the value revision control offers during the debugging process. There are many software tools to help manage this process. Although they all serve the same basic function, they can work in surprisingly different ways.

One common feature is *file locking*. It comes into its own in large development environments, in which it is useful to restrict access to a particular file to one developer at a time. If you are about to modify some code that another developer is working on, however, you might be happy to be reminded that the file is being used elsewhere when you try to change it.

An alternative revision control mechanism is *merging*. The merging mechanism enables multiple developers to edit the same file at the same time. A developer who needs to modify a particular file must first check out the file. This creates a local copy on her machine. When the developer has finished changing the file, she must then check in her changes, which is also known as performing a *commit*. The first developer to check in any changes updates the communal copy. When the second developer is ready to check in his changes, he will need to merge his changes with the changes already made in the shared copy. The revision control system automatically notices that the file was changed by someone else because it was checked out, and prompts the user to perform a merge. Revision control systems often provide semiautomatic merge capabilities for source code. When two developers work on the same file they typically change different sections of the file, and so a merge is usually a painless matter.

Most revision control systems will let you tag or label particular sets of files. This is related to the concept of creating a branch, which is a common feature in revision control systems. For example, if you've checked out a handful of Pac-Man files and made some changes to the Pac-Man source code that turns it into Ms. Pac-Man, you could label your set of files with Ms-Pacman-Branch. Then, if you ever wanted to recall that set of changes, you could. Otherwise, you'd have to remember each individual file that you changed, and also remember each version number for each file. Instead, you use a human-readable label.

Some revision control systems allow you to explicitly create a branch. The system creates a new set of files based on the original set that you are branching from. Any changes to the new branch would then affect only the newly created files.

Many revision control systems provide mechanisms to integrate with IDEs. For example, let's assume that you are planning to use Git, one of the best-known revision control systems. An entire open-source file sharing community is at GitHub (`https://github.com`), which uses Git as its revision control system. GitHub allows your repository to be shared on the Web, and it's free if you are doing open-source development. If you are using the Eclipse IDE environment that is part of the Android ADT Bundle that was discussed in an earlier section, consider trying EGit. EGit is a version of Git (based on JGit) designed to integrate into your Eclipse development environment. For an overview of EGit, see `http://www.eclipse.org/egit/`. You can find a complete tutorial about using EGit, including how to use it with GitHub, at `http://wiki.eclipse.org/EGit/User_Guide`.

Another popular revision control environment used for Android development is Subversion. You can integrate Subversion into the Eclipse IDE by using the Subclipse plug-in. Subclipse not only tightly integrates into the Eclipse IDE but it also integrates into your Windows shell (if you use Windows). To learn more, see `http://subclipse.tigris.org/` or `http://eclipse.org/subversive/`.

If it's not obvious by now, a final benefit of revision control systems is that they provide a way to make backup copies of your work. In many cases, you can automatically upload your files to a remote server. If you're good about checking in files, even a blown hard drive won't result in more than a few hours of lost time. In some cases, the actual storage can be hosted by a third party at no cost to you, the developer. You should, of course, also make your own backups of your important work, perhaps to a portable hard drive or over your own network. That way, you do not need to depend on third parties to maintain the integrity of your data.

The following are some common choices for revision control systems. We recommend Subversion or Git for Android developers, but you might already have a favorite:

- **Git:** This is an open–source version control system designed to handle large projects that are distributed over multiple repositories. It has an impressive pedigree because it was originally authored by Linus Torvalds of Linux fame. To get started with Git, see `http://git-scm.com/`.

- **Repo:** This is a repository management tool built on top of Git. You might bump into it if you are taking a look at the Android source code (available at `http://source.android.com`). Repo is designed to unify Git repositories as necessary and uploads to the Android revision control system to automate parts of the Android development workflow.

- **Mercurial:** This is a distributed version control system, and it efficiently handles projects of any size and offers extensions that provide an intuitive interface. You can download it at `http://mercurial.selenic.com/`.

- **Subversion:** Also called SVN, Subversion is maintained by the Apache Software Foundation, originators of the Apache web server, so you know it is top-tier open source. There are literally dozens of Subversion clients. We recommend you pick the client that integrates best with your IDE. You can find code and details at `http://subversion.apache.org/`.

Entire books have been written on revision control systems, so if this is a new area to you, consider buying one of them. A good place to start is *Foundation Version Control for Web Developers* by Chris Kemper and Ian Oxley (Apress, 2012). You will also find excellent resources online for learning more. If you're interested in Git, one of the best is the *Pro Git* book, written by Scott Chacon and published by Apress. It's available for free online, under a Creative Commons license, at `http://git-scm.com/book`.

Finally, it's worth noting that Bitbucket by Atlassian provides free hosting for your revision control repository, as long as you need fewer than five users. Bitbucket supports either Git or Mercurial. For more information, see `https://bitbucket.org/`.

Bug and Issue Tracking

Professionals track their bugs and feature requests. Without bug and issue tracking, it's all but certain that problems will be forgotten. In fact, sometimes an old unresolved bug manifests itself in a new way. A record of past issues is a great way to do some forensic investigation of a supposedly new bug. Instead of trying to remember what happened in the past, now you have an actual record to consult. Typically, bugs and issues are enumerated in the bug or issue tracker. It is common practice to use bug and issue tracking in concert with revision control by creating development branches named after the bug number being fixed. In this way, developers tie their active work directly to the issue or bug they are supposed to be working on.

Another benefit of tracking bugs is that it allows you to prioritize problems with ease. Some bugs can be lived with, and others cannot. But you need to know the difference before you can release your app to the public.

You absolutely must track your bugs and issues, or else you will lose track of what work needs to be done. Of course, you could always use a text document or spreadsheet. If you want to develop like a professional, however, you should consider one of the numerous programs specifically designed for tracking your bugs and other open issues. Many are hosted online where, for a nominal sum, you can avoid any installation headaches. The following list provides some examples:

- **JIRA:** JIRA by Atlassian is a popular issue tracker that integrates very nicely within Eclipse. It costs $10/month (the money is donated to the Room to Read charity) for small teams up to 10 users. If you do Agile development, its Greenhopper companion product is $10 more.

- **Bugzilla:** A free, server-based bug tracking software designed to help users manage software development. You can use your own computer as the server if you need only a small-scale deployment. Bugzilla is used internally by numerous high-profile, open-source projects, including Firefox, Apache, and Eclipse.

- **Redmine:** A free, open–source, flexible project management web application.

- **Trac:** A free, open–source bug tracker that also integrates tightly with popular revision control systems, including Git, Subversion, Mercurial, and others. It focuses on offering a minimalistic approach to software project management; it tries to impose as little as possible on a team's established development process.

- **MantisBT:** A free, popular web-based bug tracking system that is also open source. Mantis also provides the MantisTouch client optimized for smartphones, including Android!

- **FogBugz:** A commercial bug tracker, available both as an online hosted version and as a self-managed client-server version (they can be the same computer). It's free for students and small (one-or-two-person) startups. If you don't mind paying for the commercial version when you're more successful, it might be worth a look. You can find code and details at http://www.fogcreek.com/fogbugz/StudentAndStartup.html.

Finally, if you're using Eclipse, Mylyn is a great tool worth a mention. Mylyn tracks all your development tasks and integrates right into Eclipse. It works with many tools mentioned here, including Bugzilla, Trac, Redmine, JIRA, and GitHub. Some developers swear by Mylyn, which claims to dramatically increase developer productivity through its task-focused interface. Mylyn uses automated context management to integrate your bug/issue tracking software into Eclipse in a way that presents you only with information relevant to the task at hand.

Testing

New developers often think of testing as the process of manually putting their application through its paces. Although manual testing can be useful as a first step, it is not sufficient by itself. A good developer writes test cases before the creation of the application and then constructs even more while the application is under development. This process is known as test-driven development. The test cases can be written in a way that lets them run automatically. By the time your application is complete, you have a library of test cases that you can run each time you have a new release. The idea of developing a library of test cases that can automatically test your application is known as *regression testing*. Often, a bug fix can be fragile, where subsequent changes can cause the bug to recur. By writing a test case for each feature and bug fix, a developer can increase the likelihood that a regression to a previous bug is caught.

Developers often talk about *code coverage*, which refers to the percentage of code that is "covered" by a regression test. Ideally, you should aim to have a test case for each function, statement, decision branch, Boolean expression, internal state, and common method parameter value. Full code coverage represents a lot of work and often is not reached, but having a sense of how much coverage your code has is a good way to estimate the effectiveness of your regression tests.

Modern software engineering takes the concept of regression testing even further with a development process known as *continuous integration*. Although many developers might be happy simply to run their test suite before they release their app, continuous integration involves compiling and testing the complete application automatically one or more times a day. In a tight coupling with a revision control system, the most current main branch of code is automatically compiled and run against all test cases. If a newly committed piece of code causes the build to fail, often the entire team receives an email alerting them to the fault. No one wants to be the developer who was responsible for "breaking the build."

For a simple application, this sort of capability might not be necessary. Simply having regression testing at all will dramatically reduce your software defect rate. But if you expect your code base to be quite large, and particularly if the work is split among multiple developers, you might want to take a look at continuous integration. If you are interested in this sort of capability, you might find it worth looking at *Continuous Integration: Improving Software Quality and Reducing Risk*, by Paul M. Duvall, Steve Matyas, and Andrew Glover (Addison-Wesley, 2007); and *Continuous Delivery: Reliable Software Releases through Build, Test, and Deployment Automation*, by Jez Humble and David Farley (Addison-Wesley, 2010). Both are classics of software development.

If you want to implement continuous integration for your project, many Android developers recommend Hudson or a splinter project called Jenkins. See the following links for the details: `http://hudson-ci.org/` and `http://jenkins-ci.org/`. But let's focus on the first step, which is the process of writing good test cases.

Android Is Designed for Testing

As we have mentioned before, there are many benefits of programming for the Android OS. One very important one is that it is easy to write good test cases.

One of the classic difficulties that developers face is testing the UI, which can change in ways that don't affect the logic of the application. For example, an icon can move or change size from one revision to the next. Screen sizes and aspect ratios can change. These sorts of changes are very difficult to test reliably. If your test looks for a particular type of icon in a certain spot, it will break if the icon changes at all. You'd have to rewrite your test case every time you changed the slightest detail regarding your program's appearance.

Fortunately, the XML layout used by Android for UI development makes it easy to abstract away the UI from the logic of your code. Android can easily support the well-known software development pattern known as MVC, as shown in Figure 5-2. Your model represents the state of your system on the inside, and the view represents what the end user sees. This is your UI, and it is commonly written in XML during Android development. The controller manipulates the model to alter its state when needed. The model updates the view to change the way it looks. The user sees the results of the view and interacts with the controller. This functional division allows tests to be written for the controller or the model without requiring any knowledge of the view. Tests are more robust because changing the view (how things are rendered to the screen) does not break the tests.

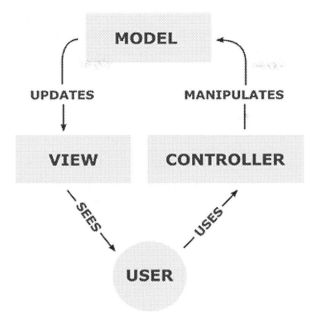

Figure 5-2. Model-View-Controller paradigm
Source: http://en.wikipedia.org/wiki/File:MVC-Process.png

Android has also embraced the JUnit unit testing framework commonly used for Java development. JUnit is tightly integrated with Android. In fact, Android even offers an `AndroidTestCase` class that is derived from JUnit's `TestCase` class. `AndroidTestCase` gives you access to a lot of internal Android constructs (specifically, the `Context` class) which simplifies test case construction. From Eclipse, making a new test environment for your application is as simple as selecting the New Test Project item from the Android Tools menu. The test cases you write actually run within the Eclipse IDE.

Unit Testing versus System Testing

It's important to distinguish between unit testing and system testing. *Unit testing* means testing a small component of your software. In an object-oriented language such as Java, it is typical for each class to be tested on its own. *System testing* refers to testing the entire application as a functional entity. Although unit testing is great for making sure that each functional component of your software is working correctly, you use system testing to ensure that all your components interact correctly. You can't be sure that everything works unless you've tested it at the system level. This typically requires that you run the application on a phone or on an emulator. Because Android devices come in so many flavors, you're probably best off running your system tests on both.

When writing unit tests, a developer often has problems when his class needs to interact with Android APIs. The Android development environment supplies an android.jar file that is used by Eclipse to ensure that your calls to Android libraries can compile on your computer. But the android.jar file only includes stubs; if you actually try to execute your code on the PC, it will fail the first time it calls an Android API. You need to run the application on your phone (or in the emulator) to have access to the full APIs.

The `AndroidTestCase` class can help make this possible. A developer can use `AndroidTestCase` to call parts of the API when emulating his code using the Android SDK phone emulator. But it can take a while to run through a large number of test cases on the emulator! Although this process can work fine for system-level testing, it can be simply too slow to work effectively if you're unit testing a large code base.

One solution is to use mock frameworks, which are frameworks that provide all the same API calls you'd see when running the code in the emulator or on the phone. But you can run these mock frameworks locally on your desktop development machine and *without* the emulator! That can make testing go much faster. Two well-known mock frameworks are Mockito and Android Mock: `http://code.google.com/p/mockito/` and `http://code.google.com/p/android-mock/`, respectively.

Sometimes mocking classes can get complicated; you have to write a lot of code to get a meaningful test. A solution for *that* problem is Robolectric. It provides a very clever system that automatically rewrites internal parts of Android functions in a way that allows you to test them without depending on the emulator. It's worth checking out when you find your tests becoming laborious to write and execute: `http://pivotal.github.com/robolectric/`

There's a lot more to be said about testing, but we have time to give you only a quick introduction. If you want to learn more about Android testing, the Android web site is the best place to start: `http://developer.android.com/tools/testing/index.html`

You might also consider picking up a book on JUnit testing.

User Experience Testing

One of the problems of developing an application, or creating anything for that matter, is that you become too close to the project. Eventually, you have to see how the application does when other people are involved. This is where you can begin to refine your app by finding outsiders who are willing to help you test it.

When it comes to finding someone to test your application, you need to find people who have not tried your app before and then tell them as little about it as possible. Try to find all levels of expertise, such as people who have never even used an Android device before. It is ideal to have developers, designers, and a handful of potential users in your group. As the old saying from the shampoo commercial goes, you don't get a second chance to make a first impression, so it is important to make certain you get their first impressions right away.

The most basic form of usability testing is sometimes called *hallway testing*. Imagine finding random people who are walking past you in the hallway and asking them to test your app. This is a good approach for the early stages of testing, in which serious issues can be uncovered quickly. You can consider this sort of user experience testing to be *alpha testing*; in other words, the first testing involving potential users or customers. As shown in Figure 5-3, there is some evidence that small groups of testers are more than sufficient, and the value of additional testers decreases asymptotically.

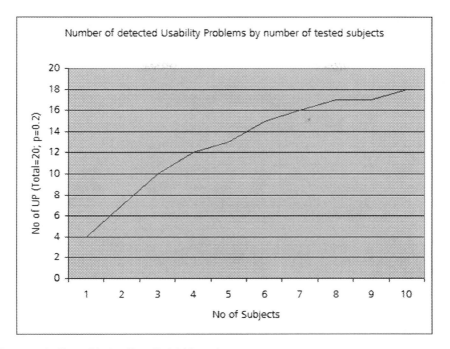

Figure 5-3. Adding more testing subjects offers diminishing returns
Source: `http://en.wikipedia.org/wiki/File:Virzis_Formula.PNG`

It is good practice to keep your testing sessions relatively short so that you do not alienate testers who aren't interested in wasting a lot of time on your test. You want your testers engaging with the app, and if they are getting bored, your results won't be as meaningful.

Often, simply watching testers work with your app without giving them any hints will give you the best feedback. But consider that even looking over their shoulder can bias the test because it's hard to fight the urge to steer them to the correct solution with body language.

If you intend to follow up the testing session with a series of questions about their experience, try to use questions that can be answered in a quantifiable way. For example, your testers can circle one of the following multiple-choice options: strongly agree, agree, no opinion, disagree, or strongly disagree. Now you can collect their answers and get an average score. If you ask the same question of your testers in another round of testing, you can see whether there has been a measurable improvement.

Beta Testing Without the MarketPlace

One important and critical part of the app development process is *beta testing*, which involves a formal release to a limited group of outsiders. Outside users are liable to use your application in ways that you never expected, and they might be using Android devices in ways that you could not test. Solving any issues before the application goes public will ensure that the application will run with fewer unexpected problems, which will result in better reviews. Of course, your beta users should be warned that the software might be buggy, so their expectations are set correctly.

Chapter 8 will discuss how to beta test using the Amazon Appstore for Android or Google Play. It is possible to beta test without ever listing your application in the public forum. The easiest way involves simply emailing an APK file to beta users you have selected. Your beta users will receive an email with an Install button when they open the email on an Android device. You can also place the APK on your web site, in a password-protected area, and users who click on the download link have the application automatically installed on their device—assuming that they have allowed the installation of apps from unknown sources.

Summary

If you're an experienced developer, most of what we've discussed in this chapter should be old hat. But if you're new to the game, we hope you've come away with a sense of the processes that make software development run smoothly.

To review, we highly recommend pursuing a formal software development methodology like the Waterfall or Agile methods we discussed. You will also want to document your code, if for no other reason than to make sure you understand what you did in the future. You should familiarize yourself with Android debugging tools, and make sure you save incremental changes to your code using revision control. To make certain you don't lose track of important bugs and issues, make sure you have a formal process for tracking them. When it comes to testing your code, we recommend unit testing with JUnit and Android's AndroidTestCase class. You should also system test your application, and Android makes both relatively painless. You also definitely want to make certain you test your app with actual users, both using informal "hallway" testing, as well as beta testing.

Here is a checklist of questions to ask:

- Are you following a software engineering process?
- Have you designed your app so it can be easily tested?
- Have you thought about appropriate tests before or during app development?
- Do you have a complete regression test suite? Do all tests pass?
- Is your app under revision control?
- Do you have a bug- and issue-tracking system in place?
- Have you done user experience testing?
- Have you beta tested before publicly releasing your app?

Chapter 6

Making Money with Ads on Your Application

Mobile advertising is on the rise! Worldwide mobile advertising is expected to reach $11.4 billion in 2013 and is projected to reach $24.5 billion in 2016. The train is leaving the station, so let's get on board!

Naturally, if you're interested in mobile advertising, you're hoping to make some money. Mobile advertising is a numbers game; the amount of money you will make per user is quite small, so you must have a very large user base before you can make serious revenue.

On that note, consider that putting an ad in your paid app is often a fatal combination because no one wants to pay for an app and then have to deal with advertising. Besides, in order to make a significant profit, you have to get a lot of downloads, and paid apps rarely reach the level of downloads needed to make meaningful ad revenue.

Figure 6-1 gives you a sense of exactly how many users you need to make money with in-app advertising.

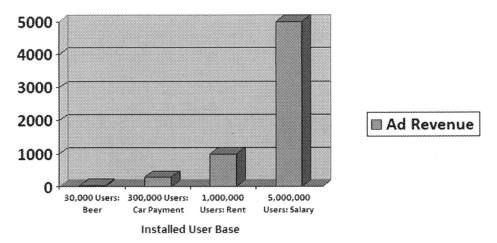

Figure 6-1. Ad-based revenues are proportional to your app's user base

These numbers are intended only as an estimate. The actual values will depend heavily on the specifics of your app. We'll soon get into the math that will allow you to calculate these numbers for your own app. That said, as you can see, it generally requires a surprisingly large number of users to generate enough ad revenue to surpass the "beer money" stage.

To begin, you will need to sign up with one or more ad networks. These networks, such as AdMob, Mobclix, and Leadbolt, connect advertisers with content publishers. From an advertiser's perspective, you as an app developer are a content publisher. On the technical side, the ad network will give you an application programming interface (API) with which to serve its ads.

We'll say more about that later, but let's talk about the types of ads you can use first.

Types of Mobile Ads

Although ads come in many shapes and sizes, there are two basic types: banner ads and interstitial ads.

Banner ads are those little rectangle ads you've seen on mobile devices. They come in many sizes and can be tailored to fit portrait and landscape modes on smartphones and tablets alike. 320x50 and 300x50 are as close as the industry has to a standard size, although new sizes are always emerging. In a useful development, AdMob (and perhaps others) has begun supporting a "Smart Banner" that automatically resizes to support the screen size and orientation of the device it is rendered to. Figure 6-2 shows an example of an AdMob Smart Banner ad. You can learn more about Smart Banners at `https://developers.google.com/mobile-ads-sdk/docs/admob/smart-banners`.

Figure 6-2. BPM Detector screen shot. This AdMob Smart Banner ad is automatically served in the local language; in this case, Hebrew

Interstitial ads are a more powerful sort of ad. They are full-screen ads and often last for a fixed time before returning the user back to the application. The specific time (generally on the order of seconds) is often configurable by the developer so the interstitial ad can fit the pace of the application. Alternatively, an interstitial might be configured to force the user to click in order to return to the application, or involve streaming video. As you might expect, they pay more than banner ads, but are also a lot more disruptive to the user experience. A common tactic is to offer users virtual currency (for use in a gaming app, for example) in return for watching interstitial ads. As another option, you could display them only on rare occasions (once every few days, for example). Be careful with interstitials; they make a lot of money per impression, but you can't make any money if all your users uninstall your app.

Figure 6-3 shows a few examples of interstitial ads. Note that the ads completely obscure the view of the application and have to be "cleared" to return control to the application.

Figure 6-3. Examples of interstitial ads

Mobile Ads by the Numbers

Let's discuss how to do a revenue analysis of the type we presented in the chart at the beginning of this chapter. Mobile advertising has a jargon all its own, and you need to know the lingo before you can make sense of any financial calculations. In Figure 6-4, note the attention given to statistics such as Revenue, eCPM, Requests, Impressions, Fill Rate, and CTR in the AdMob screen shot.

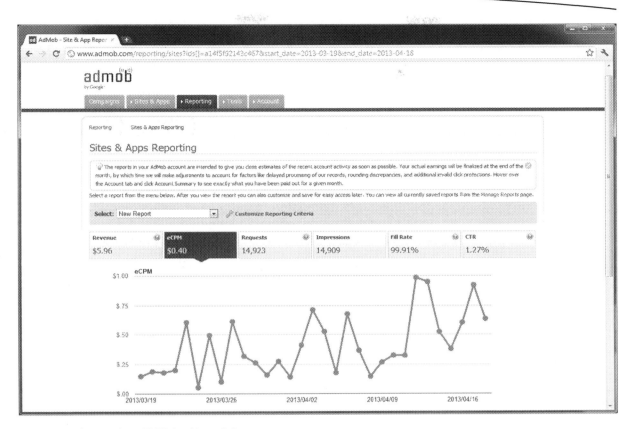

Figure 6-4. *Screen shot of AdMob with statistics*

You're going to hear a lot about eCPM, which is the estimated-cost-per-thousand ("M" is the Roman numeral for thousand, remember). eCPM is the basic metric for evaluating your advertising revenue. This abbreviation refers to the amount you will be paid for every 1,000 impressions. An *impression* is when an ad gets displayed on your app somewhere in the world. So right away, you can see that there are two key factors in maintaining a high eCPM. You need lots of people using your app and you need them to use your app for a while. After all, the longer your app stays open, the more ads will get served.

As a publisher, you will typically see eCPMs ranging between as little as $0.20 and as much as $1.25. That's the typical range, but there are no guarantees. Typically, advertisers pay on a sliding scale where payment depends on the value of the ads that are served. The ad networks simply pass on a portion of their proceeds to you, and the amount that advertisers are willing to pay depends on the market they advertise to. For example, an insurance provider will typically be willing to pay much more to acquire customers than a video game manufacturer.

Also, eCPMs can be seasonal. You'll typically make more during holidays, and especially around the holiday season in late December.

The click-through rate (CTR) lets you know how often a user actually clicks an ad that is shown in your app. Some ad networks hide these figures from you and simply let you know your eCPM, without regard to click-through rates. But you should understand that the more your users click ads, the more money you stand to make. Naturally, this means you should always have an ad available for your users to click (subject to fill rates, as discussed in the next paragraph). If your app has multiple screens, consider putting an ad in every one! You can even put an ad in the Settings screen, and we'll show you how later. But keep in mind that too many ads might alienate users, so be aware of "ad overkill." You will have to experiment to find the optimal balance.

An ad network's *refresh rate* is how often a new ad is sent for display to your app. Many ad networks make these figures adjustable by the developer. You will have to experiment to determine what works best for you. Consider that each new ad is a new opportunity for a user to find something interesting enough to click. On the other hand, if you serve ads too often, your users will find them distracting and perhaps even annoying enough to uninstall your app. Surprisingly, at least for the uninitiated, often your app does not get served an ad even when it wants to display one. The *fill rate* refers to the percentage of time your app will have ads when it's ready to show them. Some fill rates can be extremely low, and this directly impacts your revenue. AdMob is not known for having the industry's highest eCPMs, but on the plus side, if you enable the AdSense option (which serves you AdSense ads when a banner ad isn't available) AdMob will provide a near 100 percent fill rate. Unfortunately, the AdSense ads don't pay very well.

One option to get around low fill rates is to integrate your app with more than one ad network at the same time. Then you can display ads from whoever sends the ad first.

Ok, so that's a background on how the mobile ad business works. So how do you make those revenue projections? You have to estimate your eCPM. As we've mentioned, somewhere between $0.20 and $1.25 is usually safe. Now you need to estimate your fill rate. This depends on your ad network, but if you want to pull a number out of a hat, you can start with 75 percent. Your earnings per 1,000 requests are your eCPM multiplied by your fill rate (expressed as a fraction). So now all you need to do is estimate how many requests you will get and you have a back-of-the-envelope estimate for revenue.

Your requests are governed by how many users you have, how long they use the app, and your refresh rate. If you have 10,000 users, and they each use your app for 5 minutes per month, and your app requests an ad every minute, then you will have a total of 10,000 x 5 = 50,000 requests per month. With a fill rate of 0.75 and an eCPM of $0.50, you would generate 50,000 * 0.75 (0.50/1000) = $18.75 per month. That's not very much. But notice that if you double the number of minutes users spend with your app, you will double your revenue. Time spent with your app is just as important as user base size. Once again, these calculations show that you need a very large user base to make a living on ad revenue alone.

Selecting a Mobile Ad Network

There are numerous mobile ad networks that would all like your business. Each of them tries to distinguish itself by calling out its high eCPM numbers, its unique ad formats, and the ease with which it integrates into your application. However, particularly with regard to eCPM, these values are extremely dependent on the category of application you have written. The following chart, compiled using data from DoubleClick Ad Exchange makes this clear. Note that this data includes all forms of digital advertising, not just mobile advertising:

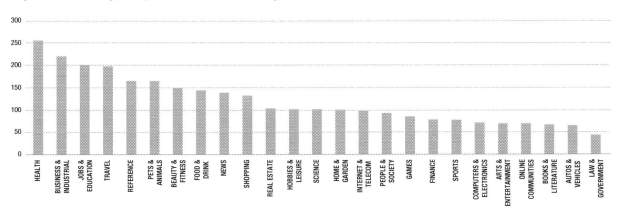

Figure 6-5. CPM Comparisons Indexed by Vertical

According to this chart, on average, an app in the healthcare space will make over five times the CPM of an app in the law and government space.

It's easy to imagine that one ad network might have a particular advertiser on its roster that generates a lot of click-throughs with your particular app because your app is targeted correctly to the advertiser. There might be no way to identify this outcome without actually trying the ad network. That said, you might be able to learn something about an ad network that could suggest it would work well with your app.

Here is a list of some ad networks for you to consider. This list is by no means exhaustive:

- AdMob: Bought by Google, AdMob is probably your best place to start. Integration is easy, and lots of people use it, so there's plenty of help available online to get started. Our technical examples will reference AdMob, but many of the other software development kits (SDKs) are fairly similar.

- LeadBolt: One of the more innovative companies, LeadBolt is known for creative ad formats that supposedly deliver higher eCPMs. It's worth a look.

- MobFox: If you have a high concentration of users in Europe, MobFox is worth a try. It supposedly delivers high eCPMs to European publishers.

- Jampp: Based out of Buenos Aires, Jampp is a leading Latin American advertising solution. It also claims to offer the highest eCPM in Latin America.

- Airpush: Airpush specializes in Android, but it's a bit controversial. It places ads into a user's task tray, which many users perceive as being very annoying. On the other hand, supposedly it has very high eCPMs.

- Buzz City: It specializes in Asia, so if you have a high concentration of Asian users, Buzz City is likely to give good results.

- Mobclix: Originally focused exclusively on iPhone, Mobclix now also supports Android. It supposedly has a high eCPM, and offers video ads and other nonstandard formats.

AdMob

If you're going to start somewhere, you might as well start with AdMob. Let's walk you through the process of using its ad-hosting SDK. Figure 6-6 shows the AdMob home page.

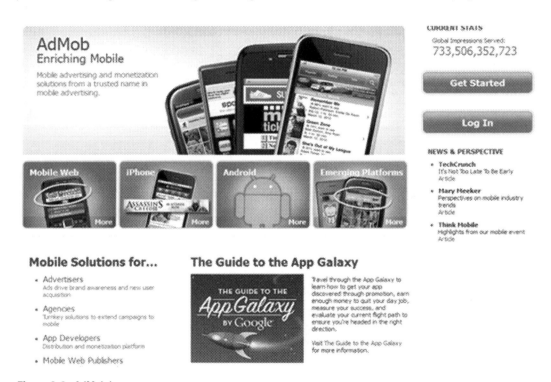

Figure 6-6. AdMob home page

AdMob's web site is at http://www.admob.com/. When Mark visited the site, AdMob identified him from his Gmail account, which makes sense because it is owned by Google. If you don't have a Gmail account, you can also log in directly to its site. Not only is the Android area good, but you might want to check out The Guide to the App Galaxy. Registration is simple, and you will receive a confirmation email that includes a number of useful links. In particular, you should see a link to the AdMob help center (http://helpcenter.admob.com/).

The help center is a great place to start learning about AdMob. If you click on the "Publishers" section in the help center, you will find lots of useful introductory material, including how to get started, how to add ads to your app, and how payments work. Remember that Admob considers you to be a publisher, since you will be "publishing" their ads in your app.

Advertisers can also find information in the help center. Just as a backgrounder, the advertiser will start a campaign that specifies how its ads will be presented on applications. The advertisers enter in a start date, end date, budget, and delivery method. They will then be asked to choose an ad group to meet advertising goals and will be given the opportunity to add multiple ad groups. They can then customize which devices they want it on, not to mention the countries or operators they want targeted. Advertisers can even customize the user demographic. Advertisers can run a Text Ad Unit or a Banner Ad Unit, and they can design them as they see fit. The ads will then begin to run, and advertisers can monitor the campaign's performance.

Okay, that's how it works for advertisers, but let's get back to you, the developer. For app integration, follow these steps:

1. Register and/or log in at `http://www.admob.com/`.

2. Click Sites and Apps.

3. Click Add Site/App.

4. Provide the information about the Android application.

5. Download the SDK.

6. While the SDK is downloading, head back to the Sites & Apps tab, hover over your app, and click the Manage Settings button that appears. Near the top of the page that appears is a long hexadecimal number named Publisher ID. Copy that number and paste it somewhere. You'll need it later in an XML layout file so that your app can let AdMob know who you are.

7. You can also take a moment to explore the AdMob dashboard. You'll be spending a lot of time on the Sites & Apps tab. This tab shows you your revenue for all your apps, as well as your eCPM and fill rates. It also allows you to view your revenue trends over time.

8. After the SDK has finished downloading, extract the zip file into a new directory. The directory now contains the AdMob library, which you need to link into your application.

9. To do that, right-click in the left-side Package Explorer pane in Eclipse. Click Properties and then click the Java Build Path property. In the Java Build Path section, click the Library tab. Now just add the JAR file you previously unzipped into the directory.

10. Now move over to the Order and Export tab. You should see the AdMob JAR file listed there. Make sure it is selected and move it to the top of the list for good measure. This makes sure that AdMob is first in the build path so we don't get any dependency issues.

11. Once the AdMob JAR file is added to the project, you'll need to grant your application all the permissions required by AdMob. You might already be using these or other permissions in your app's manifest file, but be sure you've got at least the following permissions:

```
<uses-permission android:name="android.permission.INTERNET"/>
and
<uses-permission android:name="android.permission.ACCESS_NETWORK_STATE"/>
```

12. You'll also need to reference the AdMob activity in your application's manifest file. Place the following within the application tag in the manifest .xml file:

```
<activity android:name = "com.google.ads.AdActivity"
          android:configChanges = "screenSize|smallestScreenSize|keyboard|keyboardHidden|
orientation|screenLayout|uiMode"/>
```

13. That lets your app know you'll be using the AdMob activity. You'll want to display the ad in at least one layout, and ideally in enough layouts so the ad is always visible to your users. Within each layout, the ad is simply a view, aptly named AdView. Here's an example of an AdView layout element:

```
<RelativeLayout
    [...]
    xmlns:ads="http://schemas.android.com/apk/lib/com.google.ads"
[...]
<com.google.ads.AdView
        android:id="@+id/adView1"
        android:layout_width="wrap_content"
        android:layout_height="wrap_content"
        ads:adUnitId="1234567890abcde"
        ads:adSize="BANNER"
        ads:loadAdOnCreate="true"/>
```

14. Notice the adUnitId tag. That number is the publisher ID we discussed earlier. That's it! You should now have ads enabled in your app. It might take a few minutes before you're served your first ad, so be a little patient. An example of an application hosting AdMob is shown in Figure 6-7.

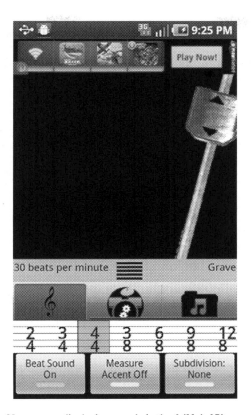

Figure 6-7. *The Sandberg Sound Free Meganome, displaying an ad via the AdMob API*

With AdMob comes AdWhirl, which was acquired by AdMob. AdWhirl is an open–source ad mediation tool that allows its users to monetize inventory as effectively as possible. Users can allocate inventory to House Ads, AdMob ads, and ads from other networks.

Mobclix

In Mobclix's own words, it is "the industry's largest mobile ad exchange network via its sophisticated open marketplace platform and comprehensive account management solution for iPhone application developers, advertisers, ad networks, and agencies." Don't let the word "iPhone" put you off from giving Mobclix a try because it also works on other platforms such as Android. Mobclix works with many ad networks, as you can see from its web site (see Figure 6-8).

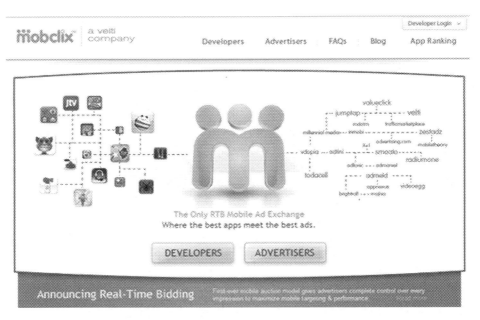

Figure 6-8. Home page for Mobclix at `http://mobclix.com/`

The company boasts the highest eCPMs and claims that its monthly infographics can reveal insight on user behavior, so that you can lay out a more thoughtful ad campaign.

Signing up for Mobclix is simple, and it is equally simple to register one's applications. Mark found that when I signed up, I got a confirmation e-mail that stated I had to "integrate Mobclix SDK into my app and submit to iTunes." I found that odd because I wanted to get started with Android.

I found that you should be able to download the Mobclix Android SDK at `http://groups.google.com/group/mobclix-android-sdk?pli=1` for the latest release. From there, you can use its 100–percent fill rates and analytics to start making money.

Affiliate Programs

Although not precisely mobile ads, affiliate programs are similar in that you use your app to direct users' eyes to mobile websites. The idea of an affiliate program is that an advertiser encourages a developer to send traffic to its retail sale web site, and a minute commission fee is given out for sales rendered. As someone who has done a little work on the web, Mark occasionally receives some revenue with affiliate programs such as Amazon. They are pretty easy to sign up for and set up, and it is possible to use these same affiliates from within an Android app.

Beyond individual affiliates such as Amazon, you can also find affiliate networks. These companies do for affiliates what ad networks do for advertisers. In other words, they connect affiliates with publishers. Instead of an ad, a link to the affiliate's web site is provided, and payment occurs when a purchase occurs. In a sense, an affiliate network is a kind of ad network in which payment occurs only if a sale is made on the referral.

You should weigh the benefits of an affiliate program versus a typical ad network. Ad networks are more common in mobile apps and they are generally easier to integrate into your application. Although affiliate programs make more money per transaction, it is harder to close a sale than it is merely to get eyes on a web site. In other words, it's likely that affiliate marketing will make sense only if something about your app makes it very likely that the user will close a sale with your affiliate. For example, if you have a music player app, perhaps referrals to a hardware provider that sells great speakers for Android phones would result in a high rate of sales conversions.

Rakuten Linkshare (at `http://mthink.com/affiliate/`) is the top affiliate network in the world. Although it doesn't have an API specific to Android, it can be called from within an Android application using an HTML API. This is the same way a publisher links with an affiliate on the web. Rakuten Linkshare has tested its service with a number of mobile platforms, including Android. To learn more, visit its web site at `http://www.linkshare.com/advertisers/publishers/`.

There are many other affiliate networks. To see a few, you can investigate the following sites:

▓ Commission Junction: `http://www.cj.com`

▓ ClickBank: `http://clickbank.com`

▓ ShareASale: `http://shareasale.com`

▓ AvantLink: `http://avantlink.com`

▓ RevenueWire: `http://revenuewire.com`

Even though Amazon isn't an affiliate network, its sheer size makes it the third largest affiliate service. You can learn about Amazon's affiliate program at `https://affiliate-program.amazon.com/gp/associates/join/landing/main.html`. eBay also has a large affiliate service. You can learn about it at `https://ebaypartnernetwork.com/files/hub/en-US/index.html`.

A recent announcement by AdMobix is allowing ads to be integrated into an Android application. It seems to be one of the few affiliate networks with an SDK specifically designed for Android. This SDK allows advertisements to be integrated in the application between levels, page loads, or anywhere on the page.

The AdMobix program has a Pay Per Install option that allows developers and advertisers to gain additional users, paying only when their product is installed on a customer's device, as opposed to paying per view or by click. Other options include Pay Per Call and Pay Per Lead.

You can find more information at the AdMobix SDK for Android site at `http://blog.adcommunal.net/admobix-sdk-for-android`. At the time of this writing, it currently is in beta.

Figure 6-9 shows the e-mail address to sign up for the beta version of the AdMobix SDK for Android.

AdMobix SDK for Android

We are proud to announce that we have just taken AdMobix to the next level!
The brand new AdMobix SDK for Android is now available for beta testers.

It includes:

» A dynamic banner rotator to place in your App

» Configurable refresh intervals

» Interface that allows you to select the campaigns you want to run on your App

Very easy to install: simply include the JAR-File in your Android project, specify your Affiliate ID, place the rotator in your layout and you are all set to monetize your App!

To apply as a beta tester, please email beta@adcommunal.com.

Figure 6-9. *E-mail address to sign up for the beta version of the AdMobix SDK for Android, an affiliate program for Android applications*

We wouldn't be surprised if Android affiliate markets grow more in the near future. If there is one thing we have learned from business on the Internet, it is that someone usually makes a product if enough people clamor for it.

Technical Tricks

One very useful trick to improve your ad revenue is to place an ad in every screen of your app. Many apps have a Settings screen where user preferences are selected.

Figure 6-10 shows a screen shot of Free Meganome with an ad in the Settings screen.

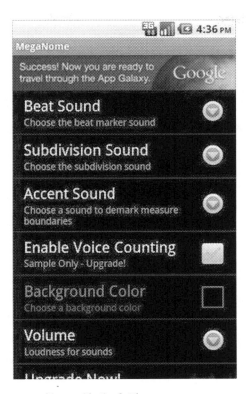

Figure 6-10. *Screen shot of Free Meganome with an ad in the Settings screen*

Android provides a standard framework for Preferences, and your ads can be made to work with that framework. First, you will need a custom preference that supports ads. Note that the following example extends Preference, a technique that has been deprecated in Android 3.0 in favor of PreferenceFragment. This example continues to use Preference to support the roughly 40 percent of the market that isn't using Android 3.0 or newer. If you are targeting only Android 3.0 and later, you should consider modifying your code to follow the example found here: http://developer.android.com/reference/android/preference/PreferenceActivity.html

```
public class AdmobPreference extends Preference
{
    public AdmobPreference(Context context) {
        super(context, null);
    }
    public AdmobPreference(Context context, AttributeSet attrs) {
        super(context, attrs);
    }
    @Override
    protected View onCreateView(ViewGroup parent) {
            //override here to return the admob ad instead of a regular preference display
```

```
        LayoutInflater inflater = (LayoutInflater) getContext().getSystemService
(Context.LAYOUT_INFLATER_SERVICE);
        return inflater.inflate(R.layout.admob_preference, null);
    }
}
```

This custom preference simply looks for an admob_preference layout to inflate. That's where all the work is done. The .xml file (minus the XML header) is reproduced here (notice the familiar AdView layout contained within):

```
<RelativeLayout
    xmlns:android="http://schemas.android.com/apk/res/android"
    xmlns:ads="http://schemas.android.com/apk/lib/com.google.ads"
    android:layout_width="fill_parent" android:layout_height="fill_parent"
    >
            <com.google.ads.AdView
            android:id="@+id/adView1"
            android:layout_alignParentTop="true"
            android:layout_centerHorizontal="true"
            android:adjustViewBounds="true"
        android:layout_width="wrap_content"
        android:layout_height="wrap_content"
        ads:adUnitId="1234567890abcde"
        ads:adSize="BANNER"
        ads:loadAdOnCreate="true"/>
</RelativeLayout>
```

That's it! Those two files are all you need. Simply place your AdmobPreference into your existing list of preferences and you'll have ads in your Preferences screen!

Summary

If you have the right kind of app, advertising is a great way to make money. Remember, the ideal app for advertising is one that is used frequently and in which each session of use will last a while. That's because your ad revenue is proportional to the number of ads served. Regardless of the specifics of your app, you can maximize your ad revenue by making sure there's an ad on every screen in your app. We've shown you how to add an ad into the preferences screen, so be sure and do at least that. You can also consider experimenting with interstitial ads, but be sure they make sense in your app, or else you could alienate users. Finally, be sure to experiment with different ad networks.

Here is a checklist for working with in-app ads:

▓   Have you made ad revenue projections, and do they meet your expectations?

▓   Have you selected one or more ad networks?

▓   Have you selected the type of ad that works best for your app?

Chapter 7

In-App Billing: Putting a Store in Your Application

In-app billing allows a developer to charge users for app features after their app has already been downloaded. Imagine charging users for more levels of your game or charging them for virtual goods (such as a magic sword in a game). For non-gaming apps, you could charge for special features or even per use if the use case is strong enough.

One example of in-app billing is Comics, by Comixology (see Figure 7-1). Comics is an application that is designed to give Android smartphone and tablet users access to digital versions of their favorite comic books. Downloading the application is free, but most of the comics cost the user. We're sure that Comixology had to make some sort of deal with the comic book companies in order to offer this service, but after those companies receive their share of the profits, we're also sure that Comixology makes a healthy profit from comic book readers paying for digital comic book content. All that is required of the user is to create an account online, and it syncs up very well.

Figure 7-1. *A screenshot from the store at Comixology, in which users can purchase their favorite digital comic books in digital form*

Tap Tap Revenge also uses the same kind of marketing in order to sell tracks. Tap Tap Revenge (see Figure 7-2) is a music game in which players tap the screen to the rhythm of their favorite tunes. The game offers a few songs for free, but if you want more, you have to pay. We're sure that the music industry gets its percentage along with the developers.

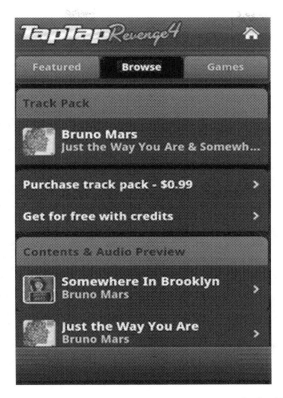

Figure 7-2. Tap Tap Revenge 4 uses in-app billing so the user can purchase more tracks for this music-based game

Many gaming applications, such as Tap Tap Revenge, have a sort of token economy that allows the user to play the game and then use their points or coins earned within the game to buy bonuses.

In Gun Brothers (see Figure 7-3), the user has the opportunity to play a shooting game and earn a lot of points. These points can be used to purchase gun upgrades, and so forth. If the user wants to take a shortcut and just buy the upgrades, however, he or she is more than welcome to do that thanks to in-app billing.

Figure 7-3. The in-app billing on Gun Brothers from Glu Mobile allows the user to buy War Bucks or Coins that can be used for armor, weapons, or power-ups

You may be surprised that there is a market for this type of gaming virtual goods, but people routinely pay money for game bonuses. This is the beauty of gaming applications; there are many gamers who are willing to lay their money down for things that exist only in a virtual gaming world. That certainly is a positive trend for developers.

In-App Market Players

If you want to use in-app billing, the Google Play Store is not the only game in town. Amazon is perhaps the best-known alternative, and there are others that we will discuss later in this chapter.

For now, we'll talk briefly about the Google Play Store and the Amazon Appstore because they are the two largest players. In general, all in-app stores take 30 percent of your list price as their transaction fee for in-app purchases. This matches the transaction fee for app stores in general. As you can see, the main reason to use in-app stores other than the Play Store is not the transaction fee.

In fact, the main reason you'll end up using other in-app stores is simply a matter of compatibility. Amazon doesn't let you use anyone else's in-app billing on apps downloaded from its store. Likewise, Google doesn't let you use anyone else's billing on apps downloaded from the Play Store. Smaller marketplaces such as SlideME have more permissive rules, but you generally have to support multiple in-app billing providers if your app needs in-app billing, and you plan to list your app in multiple marketplaces.

You might wonder why you'd even want to bother with the smaller app stores. The thing to remember is that some of these lesser-known app stores have exclusive deals or have a very high profile with certain devices. For example, the Amazon Appstore is the exclusive app store for all Kindles, which make up 33 percent of U.S. Android tablet sales. If your app works well on tablets, you give up a large part of the market if you don't list your app on Amazon.

Likewise, the Samsung apps store is preinstalled on almost all Samsung Android devices. SlideME is the exclusive app store on more than 20 million Android devices. Nook Apps is the exclusive app store on all NOOK tablets, which make up 10 percent of the U.S. tablet market.

So not only do many of these app stores cater to a sizable audience but if you take the time to place your app in their ecosystem, you also have less competition than in the Google Play Store, and hence more visibility in that market.

We'll have more to say about Google Play versus the Amazon Appstore later in the chapter, but for now, here is a bit of information on some of the other players.

GetJar

GetJar (`http://developer.getjar.com`) is the largest independent cross-platform app store. It is also well known for operating the largest virtual currency on Google Play (Getjar Gold, available to more than 100 million users). If you want to get information on developing in-app purchases using the GetJar app store, you can find it here: `https://developer.getjar.com/android/getjar-app-commerce-solutions/`

SlideME

SlideME (`http://www.slideme.org`) powers more than 140 Original Equipment Manufacturers (OEMs) preloaded with the slideME market. Conveniently for developers, the SlideME app store supports all in-app billing solutions other than Google Play and Amazon. Its developer site is here: `http://slideme.org/developers`

Samsung Market

As the number one smartphone brand, Samsung (`http://apps.samsung.com/`) offers a large market for Android applications, with support in more than 60 countries. Its in-app purchase library is called Plasma. Developers can learn more here: `http://developer.samsung.com/android/tools-sdks/In-App-Purchase-Library`

Blackberry Market

Android apps can be repackaged for the Blackberry 10 and Blackberry Tablet operating systems. Use of the Blackberry market (`http://appworld.blackberry.com`) assumes that you have ported your app to the Blackberry platform using the BlackBerry Runtime for Android. After you do that, you get access to in-app payments through Blackberry World. You can find more information here: `http://developer.blackberry.com/android/apisupport/apisupport_inapp_payments_support.html`

Nook/Fortumo

The Nook e-reader by Barnes and Nobles has an app store (`http://fortumo.com/nook`); and in partnership with Fortumo (a payment processing company), Nook has very recently begun offering in-app billing. You can learn more here: `http://fortumo.com/countries`

SK T Store

The SK T store (`http://www.skplanet.com/Eng/services/Tstore.aspx`) bills itself as Korea's number one mobile contests open store. It has more than 18 million users and supports in-app billing. Its developer web site is here: `http://dev.tstore.co.kr/devpoc/main/main.omp`

Google Play Store versus Amazon Appstore

The Google Play Store supports both in-app purchases and subscriptions, so you can generate a recurring revenue stream. The Amazon Appstore also supports in-app purchasing and subscriptions.

Neither Google nor Amazon allow you to use in-app billing to sell real physical products, personal services, or anything else that requires physical delivery. To do that, you need to host your own store. For example, you could link your app to an online store you created with `http://www.shopify.com` or an equivalent provider. This isn't all that difficult; just link to your store from within your app. Alternatively, you could integrate the PayPal SDK into your app. You can read more about doing so here: `http://androiddevelopement.blogspot.co.il/2011/04/adding-paypal-payment-in-android.html`

If you use Amazon, you benefit from the ubiquity of Amazon's one-click payment system. Furthermore, Amazon's Kindle e-books are all Android-enabled devices. If your app is a particularly good fit as an app on the Kindle, you should give the Amazon market extra consideration. Amazon's solution may also be a bit easier to implement than the Google Play solution.

Realize, however, that Amazon in-app billing can't be used within apps that have been downloaded from the Google Play Store. Likewise, Google Play in-app billing can't be used within apps that have been downloaded from the Amazon Appstore. The Google Play Store is much more commonly used than the Amazon Appstore, so you're likely to get many more downloads if you place your app there. On the other hand, there is some evidence that the Amazon Appstore generates higher revenue totals for in-app purchases.

Some developers have refused to settle for one or the other, and have implemented apps that use both in-app billing solutions, depending on where the app has been downloaded from. At the moment, that is the best (although also the most complicated) solution available. If you go that route, there are some open source helper functions that make it easier to write software that concurrently supports multiple app stores. This link details their use: `http://www.techrepublic.com/blog/app-builder/juggling-in-app-purchasing-from-multiple-markets/1824`

When Should You Use In-App Purchasing?

Now that you are familiar with the players of the in-app purchase markets, let's think about when you should and shouldn't use in-app purchasing.

When to Use In-App Purchasing

▓ When your app offers something really valuable, but you need to give your users a chance to realize that it's worth the price. Like the freemium business model, you can let users try your app for free, but now you can get a continuous revenue stream each time they purchase something in your app. But remember that this works only if your users see the value in what you're selling.

▓ When you have lots of related ideas for your app, but you want to start with just the first one. You can keep adding content to your existing app and charging for each piece of new content. Compare this with building lots of separate apps— they would each need to develop a user base on their own.

▓ When you're offering a service that makes sense to subscribe to. Maybe you're hosting content for your users, and it's easy to justify an ongoing cost to them because you incur an ongoing cost to host their content.

When Not to Use In-App Purchasing

▓ In-app purchasing can be complicated to implement well. You need to do a lot of testing to be sure everything works right. Users will complain, loudly and rightfully, if they hand over money and things don't work as expected. You will definitely want to consider targeting your app to Android version 2.2 and higher, which supports the simplified version 3.0 of Google's in-app purchasing application programming interface (API). Fortunately, this includes nearly 98 percent of the Android user base.

▓ More user support is needed as compared with other business plans. Users might not be familiar with the in-app purchase process, so expect to spend more time answering their questions.

▓ Some users may be upset that your "free app" requires payments for additional features. This could result in bad reviews. You must be careful to fully explain this before they even download the app.

Requirements for In-App Purchasing

If you choose to implement in-app billing, there are a number of requirements. For Google Play in-app billing:

▓ You must have a Google Wallet Merchant account. This is where the revenue from user purchases will be placed.

▓ Android 1.6 or higher is required for version 2.0 of the in-app purchasing API. The easier-to-use and more-powerful version 3.0 of the API requires Android 2.2.

▓ You can sell only digital content. This means you can't sell physical goods, personal services, or anything that requires physical delivery to your end user.

- Your users must have an active network connection in order to purchase in-app goods.

- You must deliver the content; Google does not provide integrated content delivery services. In many cases, you can simply build the extra content into your app to begin with and just expose the extra features after the user has purchased the right to access them.

For the Amazon in-app purchasing API:

- Android version 2.3.3 is required.

- You can sell only digital content. This means you can't sell physical goods, personal services, or anything that requires physical delivery to your end user.

- Your users must have an active network connection in order to purchase in-app goods.

- You must deliver the content; Amazon does not provide integrated content delivery services. In many cases, you can simply build the extra content into your app to begin with and just expose the extra features after the user has purchased the right to access them.

Product Types

As already mentioned, both Google and Amazon support purchases and subscription-based models. Purchases can also be consumed in Google's version 3.0 API and in the Amazon API. For example, perhaps you want users of your first-person shooter to buy extra lives, and those lives can be consumed during game play. Subscriptions can be renewed monthly or annually when using the Google API. Amazon allows renewals to occur weekly, biweekly, monthly, bimonthly, quarterly, semiannually, or annually.

Managed in-app products are products that have their ownership tracked by Google's servers. Google stores the ownership status of these items so that your app can access them each time it is run. If the product is something that can be consumed, your app must alert the Google servers that the product has been used. This same capability is available through the Amazon service, although storing product state is the developer's responsibility. If you purchase what is known as "entitled content," the Amazon servers perpetually reflect your users' right to use the content. This is the case for access to new levels of a game, for example. On the other hand, if your content can be consumed, your app still initiates the purchase, but Amazon does not record it as entitled content. You need to track usage of the product internally and simply request another purchase when it has run out. Of course, if your app does not correctly record the state of the consumable purchase, a user could lose access to it.

Delivering Your Own Content

You may have noticed that both Amazon and Play in-app billing require you to deliver your own content. When your customers' in-app billing purchase goes through, they expect some new feature or content to appear. If you have already built that content into the app, you can simply enable it and you're done. If you can do things this way, it's certainly easier.

There are reasons why you may not be able to do things in this manner. Perhaps your content will be generated after the app is released. For example, maybe you're planning to write more levels for your game and add them as in-app purchases later on. If so, you need to worry about delivering your content. This is typically done using a private remote server. As you can imagine, this requirement adds significantly to the complexity of your code base and cost of your app. A remote server requires some back-end development, and you also need to pay any costs associated with running a server.

One option to simplify content delivery is to use mobile back-end services. They are hosted solutions that provide developers with a mobile API that they can use to take advantage of back-end servers without actually having to deploy and maintain one.

Parse is one such service. Its basic plan is free and scales to up to one million requests per month. Parse was recently acquired by Facebook, but all signs are that it will continue offering its service to the public. You can learn more here: `https://www.parse.com/products/data`

Other mobile backend services include the following:

- Kinvey (`http://www.kinvey.com`).
- AWS SDK for Android (`http://aws.amazon.com/sdkforandroid/`).
- StackMob: (`https://www.stackmob.com/`).

Integrating Your App with the Google API

Google Play offers great online help to help you implement in-app billing in your application. A good place to start is with its sample application, which gives you a working model to start from. To get started with its sample application, go here:

`http://developer.android.com/training/in-app-billing/preparing-iab-app.html#GetSample`

The old version 2.0 API included a sample app called Dungeons. In Figure 7-4, you can see the purchase screen from that app, illustrating how you can purchase a potion ("Puts dragons to sleep.").

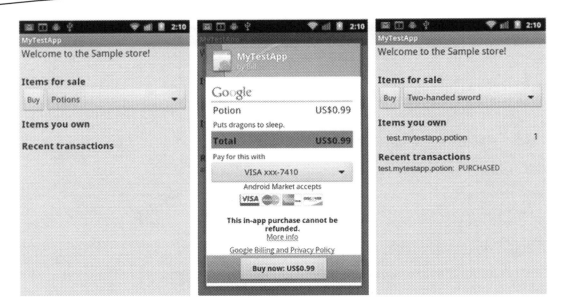

Figure 7-4. The example program illustrating the older version of the API for in-app purchases on Google Play

If at all possible, you should be integrating with the newer and simpler version 3.0 API, which uses a different sample app called Trivial Drive (see Figure 7-5)

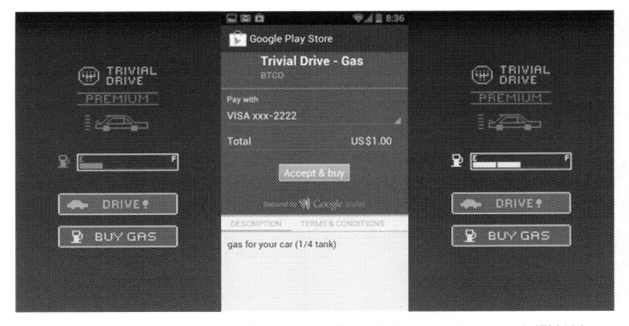

Figure 7-5. Version 3.0 of the in-app purchase API for Google Play is illustrated using an example program called Trivial Drive

As far as enabling in-app billing in your own application, the following sections spell out the steps to follow, beginning with downloading the in-app billing library. (We assume you have elected to use version 3.0 of the API.)

Enabling Your App to Use In-App Billing

To download the in-app billing library, open the Android SDK Manager. Expand the Extras section, select Google Play Billing Library, and install the Library.

Before you can use in-app billing, you must include a IinAppBillingService.aidl file in your project. This file is an Android Interface Definition Language file that defines the interface to Google's billing service.

First, right-click the src directory of your project and select New ➤ Package. Name your new package **com.android.vending.billing**. Move the IinAppBillingService.aidl class (found in <sdk>/extras/google/play_billing/ as well as the previous sample app provided with the billing library) into this package.

Add your product to the Google Play Developer Console. To do this, select your application in the Developer Console and then select the In-app Products tab on the left side. You can then add a new product. The In-app Product ID must be unique in your application's namespace. Your product type can be a Managed per user account, Unmanaged, or Subscription. You also need to add a description and price.

Initial Setup For In-App Billing In Your App

You can follow the detailed instructions here for the setup process: http://developer.android.com/training/in-app-billing/preparing-iab-app.html#GetSample

To summarize, you need to give your app permission to interact with the billing service via your manifest file. You also need to create an Iabhelper, which is the in-app billing helper class. This class enables a simplified synchronous style of communication that is one of the benefits of version 3.0 of the in-app billing API. The Iabhelper class uses callbacks to communicate with your code. In fact, the setup process uses an onIabSetupFinished callback function to return success or failure.

Using In-App Billing: Requesting a List of Items For Purchase

Again, the process is described here in great detail:
https://developer.android.com/google/play/billing/billing_integrate.html

At a high level, you need to build a list of purchasable items that you are querying. The previous link uses this example:

```
List additionalSkuList = new List();
additionalSkuList.add(SKU_APPLE);
additionalSkuList.add(SKU_BANANA);
inAppBillingHelper.queryInventoryAsync(true, additionalSkuList,
    mQueryFinishedListener);
```

As you might expect, the mQueryFinishedListener is a callback function that is called with a list of available inventory, including their prices.

Using In-App Billing: Making the Purchase

Similarly, making a purchase involves a call the in-app billing helper, and the response is handled with a callback listener function:

```
inAppBillingHelper.launchPurchaseFlow(this, SKU_APPLE, REQUEST_CODE_VALUE,
    mPurchaseFinishedListener, "developerPayloadString");
```

SKU_APPLE is the item to be purchased. The REQUEST_CODE_VALUE is a positive integer that will be returned back to the caller. The developer payload string is a convenience string for use by developers to send supplemental information. It may be empty.

Using In-App Billing: Determining Which Items Have Already Been Purchased

Continuing the paradigm, you may determine which items have already been purchased with a query to the in-app billing helper that is captured by a callback listener:

```
inAppBillingHelper.queryInventoryAsync(mGotInventoryListener);
```

You need to determine which items have been purchased each time your app restarts so your users have access to capabilities that they have already purchased.

Using In-App Billing: Consumable Purchases

To consume an item that your user has purchased, you call the in-app billing helper as follows:

```
inAppBillingHelper.consumeAsync(inventory.getPurchase(SKU_APPLE),
    mConsumeFinishedListener);
```

Integrating Your App with the Amazon API

If you've played around with the Google Play in-app billing sample application for version 2.0 of its API (the Dungeons program), you have a great foundation to start learning how to integrate with the Amazon API. This link teaches you how to modify the Dungeons application to be compatible with the Amazon in-app purchasing API:

```
https://developer.amazon.com/sdk/in-app-purchasing/reference/google-to-iap.html
```

Amazon claims that its IAP solution requires less work and has a shorter development cycle. Note, however, that Amazon is not comparing its solution with the newer version 3.0 API.

Amazon provides a visual comparison of the two APIs in Figure 7-6:

Amazon In-App Purchasing API Approach   Google In-App Billing Approach

Figure 7-6. A visual comparison of the Amazon in-app billing API and the Google Play API

Enabling Your App to Use In-App Billing

Download the Amazon Mobile App SDK package from here: `https://developer.amazon.com/sdk.html`

Extract the ZIP file into a directory on your computer. Within this directory, you find an /In-App-Purchasing/lib folder. This folder contains a JAR file called `in-app-purchasing`, which is the in-app purchasing library and must be added to your eclipse project's library path. You can do this by accessing the Project Properties menu and going to the Java Build Path. There you can select the Libraries tab and add the JAR file.

Before you can purchase a product from within an app, you must add your product to Amazon's distribution portal by signing into the Distribution Portal and selecting the My Apps tab. Choose the Manage In-App Items option from the app drop-down menu. Now you must choose whether you will be creating a Consumable, Entitlement, or Subscription product. You also need to add a price, description, and thumbnail image.

Initial Setup For In-App Billing In Your App

As you might expect, your application must be given access to the Amazon in-app purchasing library. The purchasing library is implemented as a broadcast receiver, and you declare it in your manifest by adding the following to the `<application>` section:

```
<receiver android:name = "com.amazon.inapp.purchasing.ResponseReceiver" >
    <intent-filter>
        <action android:name = "com.amazon.inapp.purchasing.NOTIFY"
                android:permission = "com.amazon.inapp.purchasing.Permission.NOTIFY" />
    </intent-filter>
</receiver>
```

Within your Java code, you access the broadcast receiver by registering with `com.amazon.inapp.purchasing.PurchasingManager`

This class initiates all in-app billing requests. To capture callbacks from the `PurchasingManager`, you must create a `PurchasingObserver` class and register it with the `PurchasingManager`. To do this, you subclass `BasePurchasingObserver`. (We will discuss each of the methods that need to be subclassed later in the chapter.) The registration with `PurchaseManager` occurs in your `onStart` and looks like this: `PurchasingManager.registerObserver(new MyPurchasingObserver());`

You also need to register the user using your app with the Amazon service. This also occurs in your `onStart`: `PurchasingManager.initiateGetUserIdRequest()`

You must implement a callback for this request in your `PurchasingObserver` class: `PurchasingObserver.onGetUserIdResponse(GetUserIdResponse)`

Using In-App Billing: Requesting a List of Items for Purchase

Similarly, a call using the `PurchasingManager` requests the list of items for purchase: `PurchasingManager.initiateItemDataRequest(java.util.Set skus)`

You need to implement the following callback in the PurchasingObserver: `PurchasingObserver.onItemDataResponse(ItemDataResponse itemDataResponse)`

Using In-App Billing: Making the Purchase

To make a purchase, call the following: `PurchasingManager.initiatePurchaseRequest(java.lang.String sku)`

The callback function you need to implement is the following:

`PurchasingObserver.onPurchaseResponse(PurchaseResponse purchaseResponse)`

Using In-App Billing: Determining Which Items Have Already Been Purchased

The `PurchaseResponse` field in the callback to the following is set to ALREADY_ENTITLED when an item has already been purchased (of course, the item in question must be an ENTITLEMENT product as set in the distribution portal):

Using In-App Billing: Consumable Purchases

Consumable purchases are simply non-entitled purchases. Once they are bought, the app must track their use. They can be repurchased at any time.

Supporting In-App Billing with Multiple App Stores

As of this writing, there is no good solution that acts to abstract away the issues of dealing with multiple app stores for in-app purchasing. However, an open-source project called OpenIAB is in the works that may change that. OpenIAB is a part of the One Platform Foundation, a global initiative to help developers submit their apps across multiple alternative app stores.

Although the code is not yet ready for prime time (or even finalized), you should track its development because once the API is released, it will dramatically simplify the problems of dealing with multiple in-app purchasing stores. You can learn more at the following web sites:

- One Platform Foundation: `http://www.onepf.org/`
- OpenIAB (Open In-App Billing): `http://www.onepf.org/openiab`

Summary

Android developers have an opportunity to monetize their applications in novel ways using in-app billing. In-app billing is perfect for selling virtual goods within the application and it works well if developers can create a subscription for their goods. It isn't for every type of application, but it is a great way to build a relationship with customers before requiring them to open their wallets.

Setting up an application for in-app billing can be complicated, both because the implementation details are nontrivial and because there is a lot of fragmentation in the market, with different app stores requiring their own in-app billing solution. Particularly if your in-app billing application is intended primarily for tablets, you cannot address a large chunk of your customer base if you don't deploy your app in at least a few different app stores.

Although there are early efforts to simplify the process of writing in-app billing solutions for multiple marketplaces, at the moment it's a nontrivial proposition, and the benefits of in-app-billing should be weighed against the complexity and overhead of the solution.

Checklist: In-App Purchasing

- Does your app benefit from product or subscription in-app purchases? Ideally, your app should be one that builds a relationship with the user, delivers significant value, and creates an opportunity for multiple purchasing events.
- Does your app meet the requirements for in-app purchasing? Network access? Digital content?
- Have you thought about which app store is best suited to your app? Will you need to support multiple app stores?
- Will you need to host purchasable content for your app?

Chapter 8

Making App Marketplaces Work for You

At this point, we assume that you have written your application, tested it, and found that things are looking great. Now it is time for your app to join the more than 700,000 apps already available for Android. How can you make your app stand out? How can you best compete for the attention of the more than 500 million Android users in the world? Let's find out.

Uploading to an App Store

In this chapter, we present everything you need to know about getting your application on Google Play and other app stores. We are going to assume that your application is running without error, which is necessary to get it on the Google Play. Other app stores might have stricter requirements. I'm sure that you have discovered that getting the application to run without errors is just the beginning. You might find that your application does exactly what you programmed it to do, but still not what you want it to do. They can be two different things.

Eventually, you have to meet your launch date deadline, and if you can't get the application to be perfect, you should at least have it running smoothly. If you don't get everything you want on your application, relax! You can always update it later.

As discussed in Chapter 1, submitting to Google Play is easier than the Apple App Store because there isn't any approval process, which means that you don't have to sit around and wait for Google to get back to you. It also means that shortly after you finish all the steps in this chapter, your application will be ready for downloading by Android users around the globe.

This is where it gets pretty exciting because you are about to have a grand opening for your application. The potential for users and profits awaits, and your application will be available for review on Google Play. You had better make certain that it is worthy of five stars!

How Refined Is Your Android Application?

If the answer is "not very," you might want to hold off on your marketing. Marketing is all about showing people your best product so people fall in love with it and want it for their own. If your product is mediocre, the relationship could be over before it even starts. Android users are a fickle bunch; even for free apps, they expect things to work well. If you are selling a paid app, even the smallest issue can alienate your potential customers. Furthermore, many app stores simply won't accept your app unless it works well.

This was the case for Mark's first application. He knew that he wanted it out by a certain time and he released it even though it wasn't completely ready. Mark added a disclaimer on the splash screen that read, "This application is still under construction. More features are coming soon. Please do not review yet."

Even though that disclaimer is somewhat unprofessional, it was necessary. The last thing you want is a one-star review for your application because you haven't finish it properly.

Eventually, Mark could make the updates necessary to alter the application, and when all the activities worked, he felt that he could take down his "pardon our dust" disclaimer. He didn't turn up the marketing until he had something to brag about.

You have to shift gears, as far as marketing is concerned, as you go from pre-release buzz to post-release buzz. That is something that we will go into detail about in the next chapter, but now we want to briefly address those who are entering the marketplace for the first time.

What to Do Before You Submit to an App Market

Here is what you want to have sorted out in advance on your application before you submit it to the Android Market:

- The application should run without any bugs. This may sound obvious, but it is sometimes difficult to find them. The last thing you need is an application that has even one Force Close window. If this kind of error happens even once, your users could give your application a one-star rating. Before you submit to an Android Market, you should test every button, feature, and activity to make certain that it runs without a problem. Ideally, you have followed best practices for debugging—including unit testing—that we discussed in Chapter 5. You also might want to do a round of beta testing, also discussed in Chapter 5.

- Test your app layout in portrait and landscape mode. Your application might look awesome, but you had better make certain that it looks just as awesome when you turn your Android device sideways. Auto-landscape is a great built-in feature for Android, but it may inadvertently distort your application's look. It is possible for a developer to turn off this feature; the emulator can show you what your application looks like in both views. Similarly, your application might look great on your phone, but what will it look like on an older low-res phone or on a tablet with a giant screen? Make certain that you get a good look at your application on a few actual Android devices and Android versions before you do an official release.

You can also change the screen resolution on the emulator when testing layouts for different devices. Note that it is possible to have entirely different layouts in portrait and landscape mode. Simply make a directory called **layout-land** under your application's res directory, and those layout files will be preferentially selected when your phone is in its landscape orientation.

▓   Make it easy for someone to give you a review. If you have a good application and you think it is worthy of five stars, make certain that the user can easily give you the rating that you feel you richly deserve. You can set up the application to prompt the user to give you a review.

Although it isn't possible to go directly to the ratings page in Google Play, it is possible to bring up your app in the marketplace. The basic code to do so looks like this:

```
Uri marketUri = Uri.parse("market://details?id=" + getPackageName());Intent intent=new
Intent(Intent.ACTION_VIEW);
Intent.setData(marketUri);
startActivity(intent);
```

Add enough logic so that your request for ratings doesn't annoy your user. Fortunately, others have built libraries to accomplish exactly what is needed. AppRate is a jar file that does nearly everything you could want. You can learn more here: https://github.com/TimotheeJeannin/AppRate

Alternatively, this little code snippet also gets the job done: http://www.androidsnippets.com/prompt-engaged-users-to-rate-your-app-in-the-android-market-appirater

If you and your company have other applications that you want to sell, you can link to those apps in the store from within your application. The technique is very similar to what we just described, except YOUR_OTHER_APP is a String set to your other app's package name, as declared in the manifest:

```
Uri marketUri = Uri.parse("market://details?id=" + YOUR_OTHER_APP);
startActivity((new Intent(Intent.ACTION_VIEW)).setData(marketUri));
```

Set up your ads. If you want to maximize your profits, make sure that those ads are in place with AdMob, Mobclix, or whatever ad method you decide to go with. See Chapter 6 for how to set that up.

If you plan to promote other applications within your own application or plan to put a market within your application, set up your in-app billing (see Chapter 7 for how to set it up). Remember that each marketplace can use its own in-app billing solution, and they are generally not compatible with each other. If you need in-app billing, you either need to stick with only one app store or build logic into your application to handle in-app purchases differently, depending on which store the app was purchased from.

Have a good description set up. Your Android application is required to have a description that is fewer than 4,000 characters. It is wise to have one that is well thought out, rather than one that sounds like you winged it. Remember that your description is a critical marketing tool. Don't be afraid to sell your app in the description.

The Screen Shot

Part of the process of submitting to a market includes taking screen shots of your app. Although app marketplaces have different rules about how many screen shots you can use, assume that you will need at least three, and typically more is better. Your screen shots should tell the story behind your app. Ideally, a potential user should be able to piece together the purpose of your app merely by glancing at your screen shots. Also, you should have a video ready (we discuss how to make a video in Chapter 9). When it comes to screen shots, you do not want to use anything that isn't pulled off the screen of the application. You need to show potential users precisely what they will be getting when they download your application.

Grabbing a screen shot is easy if you are using the official Android IDE. Simply switch your application into DDMS mode (Window ➤ Open Perspective ➤ DDMS) and run your app. At the top of the Devices pane, you'll see an icon of a camera. Pressing this button takes a screen shot for you. You can then save this screen shot to the location of your choice—you will then have a perfect shot of what is on the screen of the Android device at that given moment.

Selecting the Proper Screen Shot

We all know the old cliché about how a picture is worth a thousand words, and most Android users "read" the pictures of your application on the Android Market rather than reading the description. It is important for developers to put their best photos forward when it comes to screen shots.

In other words, don't just go through your application and take screen shots of the main menu screen. Your aim is to try and find the best visual example of your application in action. For this reason, you might not want to use the menu screen because the menu screen is usually a motionless layout of buttons. What you are looking for are screen shots that show your application in motion. If you have a gaming application, you want to show a very exciting level. The key is to tell a story with your screen shots.

For example, BPM Detector uses four screen shots to illustrate its capabilities. The first screen shot shows the default skin in action (see Figure 8-1). You can tell at a glance that the app is detecting beats per minute (BPMs) in a range between 60 and 120, and the current BPM is 60.

Figure 8-1. *A screen shot from BPM Detector*

The next screen illustrates largely the same thing using another skin, except the BPM range is empty (see Figure 8-2). Now it's clear that the app supports multiple skins.

Figure 8-2. Another screen shot for BPM Detector

The third screen illustrates "nerd mode," which displays a spectrogram of the sound data. This is yet another screen in action (see Figure 8-3).

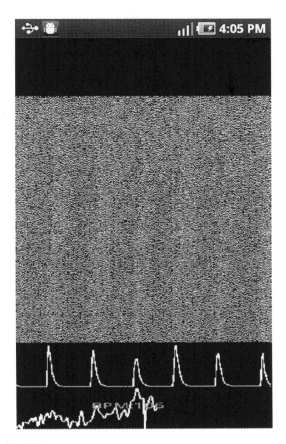

Figure 8-3. Another screen shot of BPM Detector

Finally, the fourth screen shows the preferences dialog box, which explains how you to select between all these modes (see Figure 8-4).

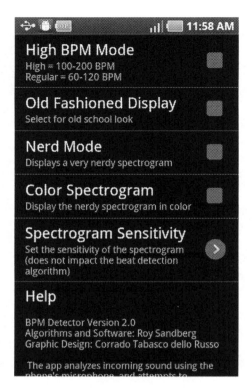

Figure 8-4. *A screen shot of BPM Detector to use as a screen shot to demonstrate the preferences option*

In general, you should think about which features you are boasting about and find a screen shot that exemplifies them. For example, if you are selling a document scanner that uses the Android device's camera, use a screen shot showing the camera view of a document being scanned, with the text "Click camera to scan the document."

Notice that you might have to alter the programming code a bit in order get a decent screen shot. Sometimes this is necessary so you don't have a screen shot that looks dull and boring. When your application is on the Android Market, you want screen shots that are visually compelling. You want a user to look at them and say, "Oh, I see what it is; I have to download that."

You also need to ensure that your screen shots are the proper dimensions and file format. The Android Market specifies 320×480, 480×800, 480×854, or 1280×800 in 24-bit PNG or JPEG. The Android IDE captures screen shots in your phone's native resolution. We plugged our Droid X in when running the IDE and got an instant 480×854 screen shot. If your phone uses a nonstandard screen resolution, you need to adjust your screen shot dimensions with a program such as Microsoft Picture Viewer. You can also use the emulator to capture screen shots and, of course, you can set it to any screen resolution you like. Unfortunately, for some applications, the emulator does not render graphics fast enough, and the screen shot smears.

Application Description

Other than your screen shots, your application description is the primary way users learn about your application. The best place to start is by analyzing your competitors' descriptions. See what you think works and endeavor to do a better job than they have.

You might want to explicitly mention why you're better than the competition. Be sure and work in any keywords that you think will help people find your app when they're searching.

If you've been lucky enough to win any awards, be sure and include them. If not, you can still work in a few quotes from happy users.

At some point, you should include a feature list, so that people know exactly what they're getting.

If your users could benefit from instructions on how to use your app, you can also include that in the description, but it should probably be near the bottom.

Many app stores don't allow fancy formatting codes in the description, so you might have to stick with plain text. Google Play is known to support basic emphasis tags such as <b>, <i>, and <u>. Embedded links don't seem to be supported.

The Icon

There used to be a dandruff shampoo that had the slogan, "You never get a second chance to make a first impression." Both in the marketplace and installed on a phone, your app makes its first impression with its icon. Remember, app marketplaces do not take kindly to flakes. Let's say that someone is browsing through an app marketplace and has found your application. What is it that they will see? Along with the name of your application, design company, rating, and cost, there is the first impression in visual form: the icon. Even though "you can't judge a book by its cover," the fact is that most people do. Not only that, they look to the icon and hope to get some idea about what the application does. That icon is more than just the square that the user taps to access your application; it is the symbol of your application. Countries have flags, companies have logos, and apps have icons.

Your chosen icon should epitomize the functionality of your application. Take the icon from the company Waze, for example (see Figure 8-5). Note the happy face, which is so well known, it is, for lack of a better word, iconic. You'll then notice that the smiley face isn't on a yellow circle, but a dialog balloon, like the type in most comic panels. You'll then notice that the dialog balloon has wheels. You may even notice the curvy lines beside the balloon, which is an international indicator that it is getting a signal. The sun is also out, which signifies a nice day outside. Also notice that its smile isn't a mouth, but something that you might see on a U-Turn sign.

Figure 8-5. *The Waze icon, a picture that says a thousand words*

What does a first-time user glean from this simple drawing? This happy dialog balloon is taking a leisurely trip—but it is not alone; it is connected. It conjures up the culture that Waze is selling: it is "a free social traffic and navigation app that uses real-time road reports from drivers nearby to save commuting time and improve your everyday driving." Even though this description (based on its actual description on the Android Market) isn't completely conveyed by the picture, it is enough to give a potential user a hint of what it actually is.

The Waze icon represents a creative approach to describing the function of the underlying app. However, most applications are so simple that a more direct approach will work fine. For example, if you are creating a gaming application called Zombie Baseball, just have a picture of a zombie holding a baseball bat. You can decide whether it is better to see the full zombie body at bat or just a skeletal hand clutching a bat. There is an actual application from Halfbrick known as Age of Zombies that uses the icon in Figure 8-6.

Figure 8-6. The icon for the Age of Zombies

As you can see, this dinosaur is partly skeletal, which means he is a zombie dinosaur. This means that you are facing a game with zombie dinosaur enemies, which are quite unusual video game foes.

Chances are, you'll probably come up with several ideas for an icon and have to narrow it down to just one.

Figure 8-7 is another example of an obvious icon. It comes from a gaming application known as Alchemy, which is a very addictive app. The game involves mixing elements (which appear to the user as icons) together to form new things. Considering the obvious association between alchemy and the use of potions, why wouldn't you use a beaker like this for an icon?

Figure 8-7. *The icon for the popular app Alchemy*

When deciding on a look for your icon, it helps to look at what your competition is doing. Please note that you don't want to imitate what your competitors are doing; instead, always try to figure out what they have not thought of yet. You definitely don't want to reproduce copyrighted or trademarked images because doing so could lead to a lawsuit. You want to create something as new as possible and to study your competition to make certain that your icon doesn't bear too much resemblance to theirs. One thing you should certainly try to do is to match the style of your icon to the overall style of your application. For example, if you choose red and black for the colors of your icon, you should probably feature those colors predominantly in your app. Having a unified style also helps when designing your logo, and you should put a lot of thought into such "trivial details" as your logo.

Google requires that your high-resolution icon have a resolution of 512x512 pixels in 32-bit PNG format with an alpha channel. You can use most graphics-editing software to output this format. Other app stores might require other resolutions.

Other Graphics Resources

Many app stores, including Google Play, optionally allow a promotional graphic and a feature graphic. You should strongly consider including these graphic resources if you can.

Video

Your video should show what your application will do as well as highlight all its nifty features. Unfortunately, it is difficult to make a video about your application when you don't really have much to show yet, unless you can work up some sort of teaser/trailer.

If you haven't done so already, set up an account on YouTube. You need a place in which you can put all your footage about your application, so you might as well do it on the most popular video-sharing site.

Making a video can be tricky, and putting up a video of low quality can tarnish the reputation of your application. If you can get a video camera that can shoot high-definition video, you should be able to mount it on a tripod and lock it into one position so you can get some shots of your application on an Android device. One good example of a company that did this is PlayOn. The video is simply one person showing how the application works on an Android device. Not surprisingly, this is the best type of demo there is to show on video. You can watch this video at http://www.youtube.com/watch?v=Ei1otuNk8oM.

Certain smartphones, such as the Samsung Galaxy S series, support video out. By recording this video out, you can make a video screen grab for use in place of or in addition to your externally shot video.

Many video-editing packages exist to help you produce a polished finished product. Feel free to use your favorite. If you are new to video editing, Microsoft Movie Maker is free, easy to use, and more than adequate for new movie makers. You can download it here:

`http://www.microsoft.com/en-us/download/details.aspx?id=34#Overview`

Multiple Marketplaces

Even though Google Play has the largest marketplace, there are many reasons to put your application in other stores. For example, you can go to the Amazon Appstore, which will give you access to a worldwide audience. The Amazon Appstore is smaller, but is growing fast. In fact, it supposedly generates far more revenue per daily user. On the other hand, there are far fewer daily users on Amazon. The Kindle Fire is a very popular device and is responsible for a lot of downloads per day, but it can't hope to match the size of the overall Android user base. Amazon is currently waiving its $99 annual developer fee, and as long as that remains true, it's probably worth giving it a go. Consider, however, that the Amazon app approval process is much slower than for Google Play. Also, the Amazon team write their own description for your app. Like Google Play, Amazon developers keep 70 percent of their app's sale price.

If you are developing an app for tablets, you should consider that between Amazon's app store and Barnes and Noble's Nook app store, over 40 percent of tablet users exclusively use app stores *other* than Google Play. You would do well to consider placing your tablet app in those stores.

There are other app stores worth considering as well:

- GetJar is the largest independent cross-platform app store and is also well-known for operating the largest virtual currency on Google Play (GetJar Gold, available to more than 100 million users). Like the other app stores, GetJar gives developers 70 percent of the sales price of its apps. You can learn more here: `http://developer.getjar.com`

- SlideME powers more than 140 original equipment manufacturers (OEMs) preloaded with the SlideME market. It supports a variety of payment processors, including Amazon and PayPal. Developers typically keep 80 percent of the purchase price of the app, minus a 10 cent payment. Its developer site is here: `http://slideme.org/developers`

- As the number one smartphone brand, Samsung offers a large market for Android applications, with support in more than 60 countries. Independent developers currently keep 100 percent of their sales revenue. That number will drop to 80 percent after their app has been listed for 6 months, and then to 70 percent after March 2015. Developers can learn more here: `http://developer.samsung.com/distribute/app-submission-guide`

- Android apps can be repackaged for the BlackBerry 10 and BlackBerry Tablet operating system (OS). Use of the BlackBerry market assumes that you have ported your app to the BlackBerry platform using the BlackBerry Runtime for Android. BlackBerry developers keep 70 percent of their sales revenue. You can find more information here: `http://appworld.blackberry.com`

In most cases, you should place your app in Google Play and then consider what other app stores might be worth your time. Once you have developed your app and have all your graphics resources ready, placing your app in multiple stores is actually pretty easy, as long as you don't need in-app purchasing.

If you have your own web site, there's another reason to submit your app to multiple app stores: search visibility. Each app store usually allows you to link back to your official web site, which results in higher rankings on most search engines.

General Issues with Marketplaces

Think about how your app will appear in the listing and how it will attract users. Most applications are found because the user actively searches for them using keywords. Make sure that your description uses a variety of keywords, but be sure that you don't simply list the keywords. Google in particular penalizes pages that simply list keywords. Work important words into your description in a natural way. If you aren't sure which keywords you should use, ask your friends to describe your app without any input from you. They might describe it in an unexpected way. After your app starts getting reviews, you can see which keywords users utilize to describe your app. Make sure to revise your description to include those keywords. It is important to pick the appropriate names as well as descriptions, and this can go a long way toward growing your user base.

Your app description is autotranslated in Google Play to every region you opt to market to. In your description, you should be careful to avoid idiomatic expressions that will not translate well and would put-off potential users in these markets. For other app stores, your text might not be autotranslated, but non-English-speaking users can still benefit from the simplified language.

Issues Specific to Google Play

The first 167 characters of your app description are the most important and should contain keywords that describe explicitly the function of your Android app. When a user performs a search on Google Play website, a 167-character description accompanies the app icon and is your second chance (after the app icon) to grab a user's attention. On a mobile device, the Google Play description is composed of the app's tagline and the remaining 4,000 characters, but before the user presses More, only 6 lines are displayed (approximately 257 characters).

Google requires that product descriptions not be misleading or loaded with keywords in an attempt to manipulate ranking or relevancy in the store's search results. Be sure you follow Google's requirements, or else you could find yourself banned from the app store.

In general, give priority to the first 257 characters of the app description because they appear prominently in the Google Market (this is what you see when you run the Google Play app on your phone).

- Also concentrate relevant keywords into the 167 characters because they are the characters seen on the Android Market web site.

- Google recommends that the rest of your description area outline the main features of the app in an easy-to-read bulleted list.

For additional help, you might want to head to the Android Asset Studio for icon generators (`http://android-ui-utils.googlecode.com/hg/asset-studio/dist/index.html`), which allows users to quickly and easily generate icons from existing images, clip art, or text. Be sure to select the Generate Web Icon option to get the high resolution icon that is needed.

Issues Specific to the Amazon App Store

Much like Google Play, the Amazon App store requires icons and screen shots. Videos are optional. When browsing the Amazon App store, the description is not visible until after a user clicks your icon. In fact, before clicking your app's icon, all the user sees is the icon, title of the app, the author, and the rating. Make sure that icon sends the right message!

A small icon image (114x114 pixels) is required, along with a larger 512x512 thumbnail image of the same image. The image must be stored in PNG format.

At least three screen shots are required, although you may use as many as ten. Screen shots must be either 1024x600 pixels or 800x480 pixels, and may be taken in either landscape or portrait mode. The image format for screen shots may be either JPG or PNG.

A promotional image (not a screen shot) that includes your app's name is required. This image should be legible after being scaled down to 300x146 pixels and should be designed to be displayed in landscape mode. The promotional image's size should be 1024x500 and must be either PNG or JPG format. All text should be at least 50 pixels from the edge. The promotional image should *not* contain pricing information, screen shots, descriptive text, ratings, or any other content that is presented elsewhere other than the app's title.

Up to five videos can be placed on the product detail page. Each should be at least 720 pixels wide and no more than 5 megabytes in size. Supported video formats are MPEG-2, WMV, Quicktime, FLV, AVI, and H.264 MPEG-4.

The approval process for Amazon is generally quite a bit slower than that of Google Play, and Amazon is known to be more selective. You can find the additional information here: `https://developer.amazon.com/help/faq.html`

Issues Specific to the SlideME Store

It is very easy to get started with the SlideME store. First, you must create an account and then you will be given the option to upload your application. You need to set a price, list your keywords (to help SlideME users find your app), and select a category for your app.

Like other app stores, you will need to include a description. SlideME asks for both a short and long description. The short description is limited to 500 characters.

If your application is optimized for phone or tablet use, you can alert SlideME users of this fact via a check box. You must declare whether your app uses in-app billing or advertisements. If your app uses advertisments, you must describe the ad network or networks you use.

A few more details—such as your software license, terms and conditions, and a privacy policy—are optional.

One minor sticking point is that SlideME parses your AndroidManifest.xml file to look for your application name. The Google Play Store quite happily extracts your application name from your activity tag (it looks for the android:label tag). Unfortunately, SlideME searches only for the android:label contained within the application tag. If this tag is missing, SlideME can't tell the name of your app and does not allow you to upload it. This is a very minor change to make, but it is a bit of an annoyance.

SlideME displays at least 12 lines, perhaps more, of text when users search for apps. Screen shots and icons are also required. SlideME has an approval process for apps that might take as long as four days. To begin, you need to create a developer account here: `http://slideme.org/developers`

Other App Stores

GetJar displays 2 lines (about 15 words) of description when users search for apps. Those first two lines are critical to getting noticed. Screen shots and icons are also required. A detailed tutorial on uploading your app to GetJar can be found here: `http://blog.getjar.com/developer/tutorial-upload-your-app-to-getjar/`

The Samsung App Store doesn't display a description when users search for apps. Screen shots and icons are required. You can learn how to submit your app to Samsung here: `http://developer.samsung.com/distribute/app-submission-guide`

The BlackBerry World app store displays a two-line (about eight-word) description when users search for apps. Screen shots and icons are required. Learn how to submit your Android app to the BlackBerry market here: `https://developer.blackberry.com/android/`

Summary

- Is your app ready to be placed in the marketplace?

- Do you have at least three great screen shots that explain the essence of your app?

- Do you have an application description that explains your app and catches the reader's attention?

- Do your icon and other graphics resources look professional and comport with all the proper formatting requirements?

- Have you decided which marketplace is best for you? Or have you decided to use more than one?

Chapter 9

Getting the Word Out

As a developer, you will find that is simply not enough to put your application out on Google Play and other app marketplaces and expect a whole bunch of downloads. Getting your application out is only the first step, and what is needed is a marketing plan that utilizes the appropriate promotional channels. This chapter discusses both the way to set up your marketing plan and the promotional channels you can pick from.

It's always good to have a plan. This chapter will introduce a number of marketing techniques you can use, but not all of them will be a good fit for your app. Perhaps you might not have the budget for the more expensive techniques, or your target market might not be reachable using certain techniques. For example, if your market is international, you might not benefit from local radio ads.

A full marketing plan is probably overkill for a company with a single app. However, elements of a marketing plan can still be useful when deciding how to best address your market.

Marketing is all about communicating the value of your product to potential customers. Before you can communicate why a customer should use your app, you should be sure that *you* understand why.

A lot of the work you did (well, we hope you did it) in Chapter 2 when defining your mini-business plan can also help you with your marketing plan. Remember when you determined the problem your app solves, analyzed your competition, and determined the target market? It is now time to think about those things in a different context. A SWOT (Strengths, Weaknesses, Opportunities, Threats) analysis is a useful way to think about how to frame your message to your customers. By understanding your internal strengths, weakness, and external opportunities and threats, you can craft a message with an eye toward your position in the marketplace. Naturally, your strengths and weaknesses should be considered with respect to the problem you are trying to solve and with respect to your competitors. Your competitors also help define the threats and opportunities in the market.

Your company's strengths and weaknesses are internal issues. As such, reflecting on your company's culture and goals can help you uncover strengths and weaknesses that can keep you on point with your message.

While competitors affect your view of threats and opportunities, so do your customers. So how does your target market affect your marketing approach? When analyzing customers, you should think about what drives their decision process. What kind of person will be buying your product? What would this person consider to be a good "value?" These questions about your target audience, which were addressed in Chapter 2, help you better shape your message to your customers.

When you understand yourself, your competitors, and your customers, you begin to understand how to best promote your product. If your app is intended for business use, Facebook might not be as useful to you as LinkedIn. If your users don't spend a lot of time online, maybe trying to get written up in print journals is a good approach. If your competitors aren't getting good traction with young blacks, and you see an opening, then maybe you should focus a lot of energy on Twitter, which does well with both African-Americans and young adults. If your app will sell for a high price, online advertising might make sense. If your app is ad-supported, you might need to resort to free forms of advertising. There are endless possibilities here, but they all begin with a SWOT analysis. Keep your SWOT analysis in mind as we talk about promotional channels. Some promotional techniques will be right for you, and some won't.

Establishing a marketing budget will help you make a decision about what you can and can't afford. We will discuss a range of marketing activities you can pursue, and many of them are completely free. Others can be quite expensive, but the time may come when that money will be well spent. In any case, you need to budget for marketing and sales costs. If you are serious about making money with your app, you should at least allocate space in your budget for a web site and some business cards. These are extremely low cost items that will go a long way toward establishing an air of professionalism. If money is tight, you can use your personal phone number for business and work from your home. Invest the money you've saved in advertising. We'll talk about that later, but let's start with your web site, which is the centerpiece of any promotional effort in the Internet age.

Preparing Your Web Site

Having a web site is critical if you want to be taken seriously. Any promotion you do should direct people to your web site, in which they can learn more about your app and then (hopefully) download or buy it. Fortunately, these days building a basic web site is easy, even if you're not technically savvy. Many online tools exist that allow you to easily create your own site. In Chapter 2, we discussed how to set up a web site for testing your market demand hypothesis. You can use the same tools to create your real web site. Maybe now is the time to upgrade to a paid account and host your own domain.

If it exists at all, your web site probably doesn't look like much at this point. Maybe you used it as a place to build your community or as a placeholder until you can get your application going. In other words, your web site may be nothing more than a shop with "coming soon" signs on it. Now you need to make it an effective selling tool for your applications. Remember that your goal is to convert viewers into app users.

Now is the time to prep your web site so it is set up to sell. This means that you will make it clear that you are in the application business. Note several elements in Figure 9-1 that show how to display an application on your official web site.

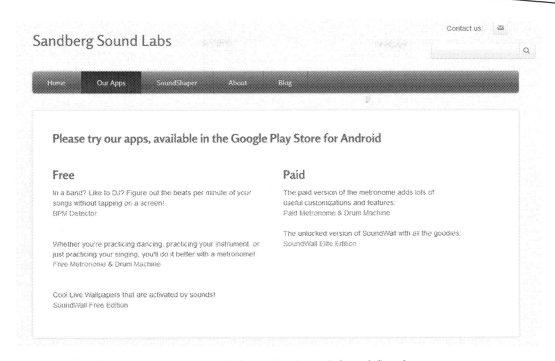

Figure 9-1. As your launch day approaches, your web site needs to be ready for an influx of users

Figure 9-1 shows Roy's web site. As you can see, the taskbar at the top makes it easy for a web site visitor to find apps. It is also set up so these applications are easily available with just a click of a mouse. In addition to the description of the application, showing the application running on a device is a convention for an application's web site. For example, you can run an image of your application running on an Android phone, but your web site can show a tablet if your application is optimized for that.

If you like, you can put a video on your site, and we discuss how to make a video of your application later in this chapter. After all, you might as well show the users what your app looks like running on an actual Android device.

If you want to, you can devote an area to listing features and include benefits and requirements. You can also put up some reviews and testimonials. For example, you can create a link that allows the user to easily share on Facebook and Twitter. We highly suggest that you create a touchscreen button on your application that links directly to your web site. Follow the example of the code there so your application users can visit your official web site from your application as well as share on Facebook and Twitter (as discussed later in this chapter).

As you can imagine, it is best if potential users can easily find your web site via a search engine. These days, the best ways to improve your search ranking is by hosting honest and useful content. As such, you will want to add as much useful content as you can to your site.

You'll also want to make a mobile version of your site. There are many ways of doing this, and you can consult one of these many sites to see how:

- Google Conversion Utility (http://www.google.com/gwt/n)
- Mobeezo (http://www.mobeezo.com/)
- Mobify (http://mobify.com/)
- mobiSiteGalore (http://www.mobisitegalore.com/)
- Winksite (http://winksite.com/site/index.cfm)
- Zinadoo (e-mail.zinadoo.com/)

Blogging

Although you might not be a blogger or even like to write, blogging is another free tool that you can use to build a web presence. A web site with relevant blog posts almost always ranks higher in search results. So we say, set up a blog! It's not hard—most of the free web site tools support blogs. As your launch date grows closer, you should blog more. The final stages of making an application are often quite interesting, and this would be a good time to start posting about the exciting challenges you have overcome.

Figure 9-2 is a blog entry from Mark's web site. Note that the way the post is written conveys that you are a human being as well as a developer. It shows that you are just trying to make something work, not trying to do something that will make money. You might notice that there are things that you don't want to put in a blog, even if they are true. You might not want to state that a certain company that you are working with is giving you a hard time because this hurts the reputation of the company. Also, you might want to avoid Not Suitable for Work (NSFW) language.

Developer Tools and GUIs

I've been considering doing my Application with some other development tools besides the traditional Eclipse IDE. I'm going to have to do a little more research in this, though. What I am hoping is that it will be easy to make my application available for other platforms, but only if we start that out from the beginning.

As for the User Interface, I am considering using some type of GUI Prototyping in order to figure out what it will look like. I will probably download several, and probably go with the one that is the easiest to work with.

With any luck, I'll come up with something, and have something that someone else can see, and know exactly what I am trying to do.

Figure 9-2. What a blog entry from an application's web site might look like. This one was made with WordPress

If you want to, you can write several blog posts at once, and then set it up so that they go live exactly when you want them to. This is a trick you can use so you don't have to spend time writing blogs daily during the week. If you are using a WordPress template, it is quite easy to do because you can schedule a date and time for your blog posts to go live. To do this in WordPress, click Edit in the Publish Immediately section under the Publish column on the right.

This leads to the question of what you are going to write about. You need to think about your company's culture and goals to answer that. Think about what your followers on Twitter and Facebook would be interested in hearing about. One good idea is to talk about the features that you have been promising. Building an application is like making a movie, and we're sure that you have seen many making-of-a-movie features on DVDs. Because only a few of these behind-the-scenes documentaries are really interesting to watch, by analogy, make certain that your posts have a hook. If you can write about creating your application in an interesting way, the blog will draw readers in.

Effective Product Launches

After you have a web site set up, you can start planning your product launch. The day your application launches will be a great time for marketing because you will actually have the mobile software to show off to members of the media. Even if your launch is really a beta release, you can still benefit from some marketing. Just make sure that you set expectations correctly. And remember that a beta release isn't a justification for shoddy software; you simply shouldn't release it to the public if your software is known to be bug-ridden. Our point is that when that launch date hits, you should have an application worthy of telling the world about.

Your launch day promotional strategy will depend on what you hope to accomplish. If you are soft-launching a beta release, you might want some publicity, but not too much. After all, if a reviewer discovers serious problems with your app during the beta trials, you don't want the whole world to know about it. At a minimum, start with your web page and announce your product launch on your home page. Post it on your blog, and generally make certain that it is known and obvious the moment a viewer hits your site.

Your promotional strategy also depends on the marketing analysis you did (we hope) at the start of this chapter. The rest of this chapter describes different promotional channels you can consider. Most of the channels we propose are free or low cost. They include social networks, online media contacts, offline media contacts, online forums, and guerilla marketing techniques. The paid promotional strategies won't be for everyone, but if your budget allows it, you can consider setting up a booth at trade shows, as well as using online advertising and traditional advertising.

Marketing Using Social Networks: Facebook, Twitter, LinkedIn

We live in the Internet age, which has many advantages. For example, if you have something to say, you don't have to make a video to be broadcast or type something up to be printed. These days, all you need to do is post, and everyone across the world can see what you are doing. However, the enormous scale of the Internet works against the lone person who is just trying to get the word out about his or her accomplishments. Any person who is into Internet marketing will tell you that you need to have a good social media presence.

Social media is a great way to get the word out on your app. It's free, and readers are already at their computer or smartphone, so they're no more than a few clicks away from downloading your creation. Let's start talking about the different social media players, and how they can work for you.

Twitter

Perhaps you're already a Twitter user. If so, perhaps you left tweets that informed the public of your app development process even before it was released. By now, you have probably found a lot of people to follow, and you should have some followers. You should then go to Twitter and make certain that you tweet the release date, allowing your followers to know what to expect—like the hype of a movie preview. If not, it's not too late to develop a following on Twitter.

Although it's somewhat difficult to work with at first, you should be comfortable with Twitter on your computer and mobile device. If you want to, you can use a dedicated client app such as Twitterrific, Echofon, TweetDeck, or the official Twitter app for Android to keep track of it all. You can even head to oneforty's comprehensive Twitter apps directory at `http://oneforty.com` to explore all manner of Twitter tracking.

You should use Twitter like you use the comments on your blog. Figure out what potential users have to say about your application and address them directly. You can then tweet about how the app is going—microblogging, a method of communication on the status of your app with short brief posts, is an excellent medium for addressing issues without giving away too much detail.

As you reply to comments, you put a human face on your product and show the world that you are not just a soulless machine whose only purpose is to make money. In the same manner, don't constantly promote your application, or you will come off as a 24/7 advertisement that people will find off-putting.

You also have to avoid the risk of over-advertising by remaining on topic. You don't want to start a whole series of tweets about things that have nothing to do with your application. It is all right to go off on a tangent occasionally, but overdoing it can lead to another type of audience—or worse, no audience.

Another useful Twitter tool is the *hashtag*. A hashtag is represented by the pound symbol (#) and is used to mark keywords or topics in a tweet. Users put a # before relevant keywords in tweets in order to categorize those tweets for an easier search. Other Twitter users can click a hashtagged word in any message and it will show them all other tweets in the category. Hashtagged words that become very popular can end up as trending topics.

The important thing to understand about Twitter and other social networks is that quality is always better than quantity. The number of followers you have is not as important as who these followers are. It is the difference between 10,000 Facebook friends and 100 true friends.

In the same manner, you don't want to just start following people so you can be followed. You want to follow someone from whom you can learn. Any Android (or even iOS) developer is fair game because you will have to deal with similar issues. You should definitely follow journalists because they are people of influence. Don't forget your friends and peers as well. Finally, follow those who are following you.

You should also take the time to retweet other people's posts, especially if they are something that your audience would enjoy. The more you do this, the more others will eventually retweet your posts. Think of it as Twitter karma.

You should take some time to create a Twitter list as well. This way, you can organize people into groups and follow them with a quick glance every day. For example, you can name one group Developers, and see what is trending in the Android development community.

Facebook

Facebook is the darling of social media. If your app is oriented toward consumers (as opposed to business users), you need to have a Facebook presence.

Be sure to create a separate Facebook page for business. In the past, a business needed 25 "likes" before it could create a custom URL on Facebook. This is no longer true, so be sure and create an easy-to-remember URL on Facebook at the very beginning.

If you already have a personal presence on Facebook, make sure to get your friends to "like" your business page. We humans exhibit herding behavior, so letting readers know that your page is popular is a great way to get legitimacy. This is known as "social proof"—people look to other people to decide what behavior is correct. If people heading to your page see lots of "likes," they will assume your app is generating momentum. Getting the word through your Facebook page is easy. Simply do the following:

1. Click your Facebook page's Edit Info link.
2. Click the Marketing link.
3. Click Send An Update.

You should use this method of spreading the word sparingly because messages like these are broadcast *ad nauseum* throughout the Internet. Before your launch date is also a good time to start using Facebook Insights, a free analytics service. When you log in to your Facebook page as an admin, you can click the View Insights link to view the metrics about your Facebook page. By studying this information, you can find out who is looking at what you are doing, which is information that will be helpful in the future.

LinkedIn

Facebook may be the big dog for consumers, but if your app is intended for business applications, you should be sure to have a LinkedIn presence. You can read more about how to establish a company presence on LinkedIn here: `http://marketing.linkedin.com/sites/default/files/attachment/LinkedInCompanyPages_5Steps.pdf`.

If you have attended a lot of business seminars or conventions, you have probably amassed a large stack of business cards. We highly suggest going to LinkedIn and running a search on contacts from every business card; then send them an Invite to your network on LinkedIn.

If you gain more than 500 connections on LinkedIn, you become a part of the 500+ club that will show others searching on your LinkedIn profile that you are well-connected. Of course, you will also have over 500 contacts that you can reach out to in case you may ever need anything.

Making the Press Work for You

The press is a great source of free publicity. Reporters are always looking for a good story, and your app might just be that story. Be sure to look for media sources that specialize in what your app does. A more–narrowly focused publication is more likely to be interested in your app and it is also more likely to connect you with potential customers.

When you are ready to release your app, you should craft a press release to alert publications that may choose to write a story about your app.

Write a Press Release

A press release is a statement prepared for distribution to the media.

An important thing to consider is who will receive your press release. As a professional blogger, Mark receives a lot of press releases in his inbox every day. Many of them come from PR firms, and some are from sites that send out press releases on a daily basis.

Use the Format for a Press Release

Press releases have a format. It isn't really a standard, but journalists get many of these every day, and they know what to look for:

- **Company logo:** You should put your full-color company logo centered at the top. If nothing else, you want journalists to at least remember your company name, so make it prominent. Some sources say the company's name, web address, location address, and phone number should be at the top, but we usually see it at the bottom.

- **Title:** We've heard some sources say that the title should be in all capitals, but it should be at least be in bold. Do not worry about it being too long, but it should be brief enough to explain what your application is.

- **Secondary title:** This is not part of the title; it is centered and not in bold. Here you can add a sentence that discusses your product in detail.

- **Date and city:** In bold, you should have the date and city of where the press release originated.

- **First paragraph:** This is a brief detail about what the press release is about.

- **Second paragraph:** This is where the journalistic five Ws and H (Who, What, Where, When, and How) come in. In your case, you should put in who cares, why you should care, where you can find it, and when it will happen.

- **Quote:** Press releases generally have a quote from someone within the company. The quote personalizes and humanizes the press release with an individual's perspective.

- **Final paragraph:** As a tech and gadget blogger, Mark always ends his articles with a final paragraph that explains the price of the item as well as any details about the point-of-sale. This information is placed at the end for immediate takeaway value, and a press release is structured the same.

- **Company description:** This is usually preceded by About (insert company name here) and then discusses the company in terms of the date it was founded and what the company does. You should then put your web site URL there.

Example of a Press Release

Here is an example of a press release for a baseball card organizer mobile app:

```
                          YOUR COMPANY LOGO HERE
```

Baseball Card Organizer Now Available on Android Devices—Allows Users to Put Card Collections on their Android Device.

Card Collectors can now take their collection wherever they take their Android phone or tablet.

SEATTLE, WA (October 31, 2011). *Company Name*, a company known for creating applications on various mobile platforms, announced today the availability of its Baseball Card Organizer application for Android. The application allows users to put their baseball card collections on their phone or tablet with the use of the camera on their Android device.

Baseball Card Organizer includes a built-in database that allows the user to photograph the front of the card, as well as the back with the stats. The user can then enter in information, and organize the cards by teams or just alphabetically.

Users can take their baseball card collections with them without taking their physical baseball card collections with them. They can flip through their cards by flicking on the screen. Baseball Card Organizer is also good for organizing other types of cards, such as movie trading cards.

"Most people who collect baseball cards have to keep them in protected cases, and they don't have the fun of flipping through them without bringing down the condition," said Jack Jackson, cofounder of *Sample Company*. "The Baseball Card Organizer gives the user the fun of perusing through their collection and not worry about getting sweat on their investment. Best of all, the user can do this from anywhere."

The Baseball Card Organizer application is now available at the Android Market, as well as the company web site at `http://www.samplecompany.com`. Baseball Card Organizer Lite is free, but the full version is for $0.99.

About *Sample Company*:

Sample Company was started as a startup company in 2010, devoted to making applications for all mobile applications. Since its launch, it has created many applications, including More Useful Stuff, Helpful Applications, and More Terrific Applications.

You will notice in the end how we took advantage of the press release to advertise other applications.

RSS Feeds and Followers

If you are like us, you read a lot of online journals. We have discovered that you don't want to spend too much time clicking bookmarks and reading each online journal or blog one at a time. Yes, it is far easier to download an RSS reader like the one at `http://www.feedly.com` and view articles in a short form, like skimming headlines in a newspaper. This way, you can find out what is trending today, and your blog or online journal should be set up so anyone with an RSS reader can see what you have been up to.

By now, you may have a lot of subscribers to your blog's RSS feed. There are ways of checking to see how many RSS followers you have and to figure out what your customers might be like when working on your SWOT analysis. In order to get more followers, you can post a link on all other social media sites such as Twitter and Facebook every time you do a blog post.

That's if you want to do it the hard way. We recommend setting up a web service such as Tumblr or TypePad to automatically put your blog entries on social media sites. It is also possible to set up blogs by using the aforementioned WordPress, as well as Blogger, LiveJournal, and Movable Type.

You should start looking at the comments on your blog. With WordPress, this is very easy to do from the template, and it gives you an idea to hear back from what will hopefully be your application's following before the application is released. From users' comments, you might get an idea of what features might be needed before the launch date or what will need to be added to after the application hits the market. You should also look for concerns in the comments. For example, if you see a lot of comments saying that the application is too hard to use, it might be a good idea to take a look at your user interface (UI).

Sadly, a lot of blog commentary is probably spam. Mark has one blog that generates quite a bit of comments per day, but half of the comments are unrelated to the articles they are commenting about. For example, after Mark writes an article about a certain gadget, some guy adds a comment like this: "Nice well-written article; it reminds me of Toupees for Men." Then there is the obvious link. Several of the comments feel generated by a machine, and they are. There are programs designed to sniff out sites and these machines have been programmed to leave their spam as "legitimate commentary" on our site. Fortunately, if you use a blog service with CAPTCHA web forms and spam filters, you can stop this spamming problem before the taint becomes an infection.

Making a Video

We discussed the idea of using a video to market your app in Chapter 8 when we talked about promoting your app in an app marketplace. But a video is a useful tool outside of the app marketplace as well. Video-sharing sites are a lot like social networks, and viral videos are one of the best marketing tools.

Plan to do some editing on your video to make it good enough to post online. You can probably get away with putting an Android device on a clean table and showing people what the app can do. As we discussed in Chapter 8, some phones also let you record video directly from their screen via a video out connector.

You can then do a little narration, but you might have to do the audio track later. This goes for any sound that your application may have, if the microphone on your video camera doesn't get it.

We have some experience working with video, and we know it always takes longer than you might think. After all, most two-hour movies take years to make. Don't make the mistake of thinking you can knock out a video that is a few minutes long in just a few minutes. In fact, you might want to consider hiring a video service to film your application if you can afford it.

Once you have the video, you should definitely put it on your site so people can check out how your application works. This is especially helpful if you have an application that is difficult to explain.

Online Forums

Online forums exist for nearly any topic. Regardless of what your app is for, there is already a forum somewhere with people who would love to find out what you are working on. LinkedIn is a great place to discover professionals with an interest in your field. Google Plus is also a place where experts congregate. A simple web search can reveal many more forums related to your app.

You may have discovered a number of relevant forums in the process of working on your app. Be sure and post to the forums when the time is right. Stay humble and treat forum readers as the experts they are–they spend time learning and talking about the sorts of things your app does. If you treat them with respect, they will return that respect, which can translate into page hits, favorable comments, and eventually revenue.

Public Relations and the Media

When interacting with the media, you need to wear your public relations hat. Although it might be tempting to simply speak your mind and let the reporter do the rest, that's generally not the best path forward. Reporters' jobs are to sniff out a story, and their idea of your story might not match yours. Your job is to steer them in the right direction with facts and figures that paint the right image.

Be sure and draft some key bullet points before taking a call from the media. These bullet points should address any concerns the media are likely to have. Remember that a reporter's job is to report on both sides of a story. If there is another unfavorable side to the information you are conveying, be sure to address it in your bullet points. If you don't, the reporter might, and he or she might do it in a way you would prefer to avoid. Reporters worth their salt will try hard to get you away from your bullet points. Consider whether departing from them is worth the risk, even if it makes for a much more comfortable conversation.

Reporters generally operate by a code of ethics, and they know that deviating from that code will seriously affect their career prospects. No one will open up to a reporter who is known to twist the truth. On that note, consider that most reporters will honor your requests to go "off-the-record." This can be useful when you want to inform a reporter about something, but want to be sure your words won't make it into publication. A related concept is that of "unattributable" speaking terms. If you ask a reporter to consider what you say as unattributable, it means that they can report what you said, but they can't attribute it to you.

Be sure and follow up with your media contacts. Often a little gentle prodding is all that is needed to get that article out into the world. One technique to motivate a media contacts is to offer them an exclusive. Use this only if it makes sense, but if you absolutely need coverage from a particular source, an exclusive can be a useful tool in your tool belt. Over the long term, you should seek to build a personal contact file with reporters. If you have any particular expertise in an area, be sure to convey that to your contacts. Over time, you might become their go-to contact for your area of knowledge. This can turn into frequent incidental write-ups for your app.

When dealing with the media, you have to think of them as consumers of stories. They aren't necessarily interested in your product, but they are interested in your story—if it's a good one. For example, Mark has often reviewed applications on his blog, The Geek Church, but the ones that have some interesting facts in them make the most interesting articles. For example, in reviewing the application Speakerfy, the developers shared with Mark that Shaquille O'Neal gave the application an award that the developer did not even enter to win. You had better believe that facts like that easily end up in Mark's articles. You should determine what facts about your app make it stand out from other apps and make certain that you tell them to reporters who want to know.

Printed Journals

Whoever said that print is dead was quite premature, considering the number of newspapers and magazines that are still in print. We are a long way from an all-digital media society, and you should take note of the local and national printed journals that cover stories about digital technology.

Mark lives in a small town, and if he needed some press for his application, he would find out whether the town paper has some sort of tech section or even one on applications. He would then check the masthead to see who the editor of the tech section is. If the editor is not listed, he would make a call to the editor and see if he or she would be interested in doing a report on the latest application for Android . . .Mark's!

The same rule applies for going to papers or magazines with a much larger circulation, but you don't want to be limited to talking to the guy in charge of the tech section. For example, if you have an application that is made for the stock market, don't you think the editor of the Investment section of a newspaper would be interested in this? As long as it is useful, the answer is yes. You should check the Sunday paper to see what sections your applications could apply to. You should also do the same for any magazines that might be interested in an application like yours.

After you have carefully revised and reviewed your press releases, you can finally send out the polished result to a bundle of media contacts. If you want to make it easy on yourself, you can simply start a new e-mail message and copy and paste your press release. You should use plain text e-mail format if you want media people to copy and paste your press releases to their articles. If you are unfamiliar with the world of news blogging, you should know that many online articles often include a copy of the official press release. In fact, Mark has worked for tech and gadget blogs that have insisted that he attach the press release to the article.

You should also include a few screen shots with the e-mail (it's easiest to just use the screen shots you used when you submitted your application to the Android Market).

You can send other types of images as well, but we would focus on images that you want to see in an online or printed journal. Every tech and gadget blog that Mark has written for has required him to include an image of some kind. So you definitely want to make it easy for tech reporters by finding an image that would be perfect for an article. Consider this the "cover" that readers might use to judge your "book" (to speak in clichéd metaphors again).

This "perfect shot" doesn't have to be a screen shot; it could be a picture showing the application in use by an Android user. For example, if you have some application that improves a camera, wouldn't it be terrific to show an Android user taking a picture with your camera-improving application? The point is that you are looking for the image that will show potential users what your application is.

The one thing that we do not recommend is attaching your press release and/or screen shots as e-mail attachments to your media contacts. Because Mark has been on the other side of the table, he is less likely to open an attachment, especially if it is a PDF file. PDF files open up Adobe Acrobat or Reader, which tends to slow down computers a bit. Not only that; having an attached PDF is often a flag for spam filters, and you don't want your e-mail to be going there.

When sending out a batch e-mail to the press, do not put all the names in the To section. If you do this, all the recipients of your press release e-mail will see all the other people you sent it to. This looks really bad to anyone who works in the media because it makes them feel as if they are just a name on a list. Worse yet, you reveal your media contacts to everyone. What you want to do is put all your addresses in the Bcc field so each recipient receives your e-mail without seeing the other recipients.

You should also look into the option of using campaign management software. These services can handle not only e-mail marketing but also social media, You can run a search for "Campaign Management Software" to find many available services, and you might want to check out Constant Contact (http://www.constantcontact.com) and Swiftpage (http://www.swiftpage.com/).

Giving Media Contacts a Complimentary Copy of Your Application

Media reviewers are more apt to review an application if you give it to them for free. Mark is a professional tech blogger and reviewer, and a product can capture his interest if its press release includes something that says, "Please let me know if we can send this to you to review." Many reviewers will say yes because they like getting free things from time to time. Just take Mark's word on that one.

Sending media people a complimentary copy is extremely easy. Simply attach your Android Application Package (APK) file to an e-mail and send away. Keep in mind, however, that your media contacts can forward your e-mail to friends and give away your paid app for free. This could be an advantage in disguise because you can ask the media contact to keep your app confidential. Let them know you trust them, and you will build a stronger more personal relationship than if they have to enter special codes to get access to your app. On the other hand, if you want to create an air of exclusivity, you can always place your APK on your web site, behind a password-protected page. This should be obvious, but never send the media any trade secret information; if you do so, it will be impossible to assert your trade secret rights later.

Even though it seems like you are buying a review in exchange for a free sample, you're not. You have no guarantee that the reviewer will give you a good review simply because he or she received something for nothing. As a tech reviewer, Mark would never agree to any deal that said that he had to give a positive review of any review model sent to him. (In fact, no company has ever had the audacity to offer him such a deal.)

In addition to giving away free samples, it is important to maintain a good working relationship with your media contacts. After all, these are the people who are doing you a favor by giving your application some much-needed press. The least you can do for them is send a thank you note for publishing your article. You don't necessarily need to make every media person your best friend, but at least establish a LinkedIn contact. Ideally, you can get them to follow your company's LinkedIn page!

As someone who has worked as a tech and gadget blogger, Mark has found that he has entered into strange relationships with tech companies and their public relations teams. There is sort of an unspoken rule that enables the company to give the tech reviewer something and then the tech reviewer publishes an article in return. Think of it as a *quid pro quo* relationship, but the reporter can give only an honest review. If the product is not of the best quality, the review will reflect that. Therefore, send out your best product to the media or suffer the consequences of a bad review that could be worse than any bad review on Google Play. As a tech writer, Mark has often received products that are so good that he has contacted the app makers to review more of what they have to offer.

Media people often get bored of looking at the same places for news stories time and time again. Sometimes they like to find a unique story and it is helpful when these stories come via a press release.

As someone who is in the media, Mark likes to have contacts who are in the know more than he can afford to be. He keeps the contact information of PR people and company representatives because they are a source for information that he may not be able to get otherwise. This book could not have been written without them, and we consulted them several times when it came to questions about developing Android applications. In other words, your developer insight could make you a good source for media people, and those media people could give you some press by quoting you. In this way, Mark occasionally contacts people he has contacted before in order to get new story ideas. Imagine that one of your media contacts told you that he or she was looking for new stories and you just happened to be developing a new application at the time. This is certainly better than making cold calls to the media!

Other Examples of Low-Cost Publicity: Guerilla Marketing

Guerilla marketing is a phrase that can mean many things, but for us it means using free or cheap and unconventional techniques to build market share. The general idea is that you develop your market by investing time instead of money. There are many "guerrilla" ideas that you might be able to work into your marketing plan.

The classic example is graffiti. Although it might not make sense for an app, if you are promoting something location-based, perhaps you can use reverse graffiti in select locations. If you aren't familiar with reverse graffiti, also known as "clean tagging," the concept is rather clever. Find a wall that has graffiti on it and then use some cleaning solution, a bristle brush (or toothbrush), and a stencil to remove the existing graffiti in a way that leaves an image of the stencil. Your stencil can be an ad for your app. Because you're removing only existing graffiti, reverse graffiti exists in a legal grey zone. After all, cleaning away graffiti can't be illegal, right?

Twitter, Facebook, LinkedIn, and blogging can all be considered guerilla marketing. Setting up a Google+ page is also guerilla marketing, and can help with your Google search placement.

Collaboration isn't exactly a traditional guerrilla marketing technique, but it's low cost and can work very well. Find companies with a related (obviously not identical) product who would benefit from your product. Often they will be interested in building relationships with other companies. You can refer customers to them and they can refer customers to you. At first, it can be as simple as linking to their web site from yours, but it can grow from there. Writing "guest" articles on other companies' blogs to discuss their product (perhaps in relation to yours) can also be a great way to build a relationship. The companies are happy because you're doing work for them, and the articles obviously add to your product's exposure.

If it fits your app's description, writing a "how-to" article that mentions your app as part of a solution to a problem is another free way to get exposure for your app. For example, web sites such as wikiHow invite users to explain how to do basic tasks. Maybe you have an app that helps kazoo players tune their kazoos. If so, you could write an article on wikiHow about kazoo tuning. You could explain the process and invite users to download your app.

Guerilla marketing requires you to think outside the box. The specifics of your app determine what makes sense for you. There are many resources online that can give you some ideas, but ultimately, your own creativity must guide you.

Trade Shows

Trade shows are never cheap to attend. A basic booth at a show probably costs four figures and that doesn't include travel expenses or the cost to create your booth and advertising materials. On the other hand, a well-targeted presence at a trade show can generate an enormous number of customer leads. Often you can tag along to a trade show with a larger company if you play your cards right. The ideal situation is when a larger company realizes that it can benefit from what you are doing. The company might consider you the cool new kid on the block and can benefit from your buzz just as much as you benefit. If that's not an option for you, you can use guerilla marketing techniques at trade shows. Perhaps all you can afford is a visitor's pass to attend. If so, you can surreptitiously place your card at places throughout the conference location. Even better, create some swag (with your logo and web address prominently displayed) that people will want. Even if you can't attend the conference, you can still benefit by determining the hotels most guests will be attending and making yourself noticed there. A great guerrilla solution is to create do-not-disturb signs with your logo and web site displayed and place them on hotel room door knobs (or slip them under the door if you're worried the maid will take them away).

Online Advertising

Advertising is the traditional means of marketing. Simply put, you're paying to get customer leads. These days, online advertising is on a tear, and traditional advertising (print media, television, and radio) are stagnant or even losing market share. Still, traditional print is not dead yet, but online advertising is on the rise.

Because your app lives in the online world, in most cases, you should start your foray into advertising by purchasing ads online. Forms of online ads can include AdWords (Google), Facebook, other search engines, ads on specific web properties, and mobile ads (including house ads). Chapter 6 discussed how you can make money with ads as a publisher, but now you'd be on the other side of the equation. You would be an advertiser who is paying the publishers to feature your ad. Remember, however, that your cost to acquire a customer is an issue. Particularly for mobile apps, whose selling price is often only a few dollars, you have to carefully consider the cost of acquiring a new customer. If you spend $3 in advertising to add a new customer, you're not going to do very well if your app costs $2.99.

A typical foray into online advertising begins with Google. To begin, you will need to buy AdWords (adwords.google.com/). The most common ad words are popular, so they are the most expensive. To benefit the most from AdWords, you need to pick words that refer to your app, but are unlikely to be used by other advertisers. AdWords supports a prepay option, which can be as little as $10. Start small and increase your payments as you gain confidence in the results. To learn more, go here: adwords.google.com.

Facebook doesn't yet support prepayment for advertising, but there is no minimum advertising budget. When placing an ad on Facebook, you can target your ad to a particular demographic of users. To learn more, go here: http://www.facebook.com/help/326113794144384/.

Other popular web sites such as YouTube or Yahoo can also be targeted for ads. But because your application almost certainly targets a particular submarket, you should try to find a web site that focuses on that group. Perhaps you have written a game and you can target web sites frequented by gamers. Or maybe you have a utility that solves a particular technical problem. Find the site frequented by people who have that problem and you have a great place to advertise. Most Online media outlets accept advertising, and although posting to their forums or writing an article for publication are guerilla tactics that can get you visibility on the site, there's nothing wrong with running ads if your budget allows it. You're developing a mobile app, so what better way than to advertise on other mobile apps? You might already have a relationship with mobile ad networks as a publisher. In many cases, the ad network can give you a discount if you run ads with their network. Also, many ad networks support "house ads," which are ads that you elect to place on your own applications. For example, maybe you already have a reasonably successful application and you have released a new application that would appeal to your existing user base. You can use a house ad to advertise to these existing users. Best of all, house ads are generally free.

Offline Advertising

Although online advertising usually makes the most sense for apps, some applications can benefit from offline advertising. Particularly if your app appeals to folks who have less of an online presence, you might be able to reach a large audience by going offline. For example, suppose that you have written an app that helps building contractors comply with building codes. Maybe you expect to be able to charge a high price for your app because it offers a useful and highly specialized functionality. Unfortunately, building contractors don't spend nearly as much time online as programmers, so they're not likely to bump into your app during a web search. You might reach them very effectively by advertising in conventional trade journals, however.

Ironically, the Internet is a great place to search for offline publications to advertise in. If you are looking for narrow niches to advertise in, this Wikipedia article lists U.S. magazines by topic: http://en.wikipedia.org/wiki/List_of_United_States_magazines

If your niche is even narrower and might be served by a technical journal, you could try searching Springer, currently the largest journal publisher. Note that Apress, the publisher of this book, is owned by Springer. Its web site is here: http://www.springer.com.

If you are looking for a local newspaper, this Wikipedia article lists U.S. newspapers by state: http://en.wikipedia.org/wiki/List_of_newspapers_in_the_United_States.

Summary

As you set up your marketing plan, you should answer these questions about key issues:

- Does your marketing plan have a budget, schedule, and milestones?
- Do you know your strengths and weaknesses?
- Do you know the outside opportunities and threats?
- Have you identified your customer?
- Does your app service a particular region (even initially), in which local advertising might be useful?
- Have you identified printed and online publications that are read by your target customer?
- Have you launched a web site?
- Have you blogged about your app?
- What social networking sites make sense for you to utilize?
- Does guerrilla marketing make sense for you?
- Will you be attending shows? Can you piggyback on a vendor or customer of yours?
- Does paid advertising (online or offline) fit your budget and your business plan?

Chapter **10**

After You Have a User Base

At this point, we are going to assume that you have had some moderate degree of success after releasing your application. You now need a way to maintain your user base after it has gone live.

Customer Support

Once your app is deployed, your users are sure to have questions, complaints, and suggestions. At the very least, you should provide them with an e-mail address so they can send questions. To reduce the time you spend fielding these questions, you will definitely want to provide some in-app or online help.

Regardless of how you reach out to your customers, you should make sure that you interact with them in a way that meets their needs. While it can be trying to continually answer the same sort of silly question over and over again, you owe it to the success of your business to focus on your customers' needs, not your own. By the way, repeated questions can be taken care of via FAQs on the web site.

There are a number of factors that will help make your customers' experience great. Customers want to have control, so they should feel that you are providing them with options that serve their interests. Nothing is more infuriating to a customer than having a service representative apologize for not being able to fulfill a perfectly reasonable request; or worse, not ever receiving any response at all. An easy way to give customers a sense of control is to give them both information and alternatives. If you tactfully spend a bit of time explaining why things are the way they are, they will feel respected. After you explain the "why," be sure to provide meaningful options. For example, if a new release has broken a feature, you could say, "I'm very sorry that the feature isn't working. Our engineers are working on a fix for it right now. The release that broke the feature wasn't fully tested on your phone because our test team didn't have access to it. If you want a complete refund, I completely understand. If you prefer, we can upgrade you to the latest version at no cost as soon as it becomes available."

Maintaining a friendly demeanor is common sense, but it's easy to forget this when you're under pressure and dealing with an angry customer. Just as jujutsu is a martial art that seeks to turn an opponent's strengths against them, you can use emotional jujutsu when faced with an angry customer. If you actively empathize with a customer's anger ("You seem very angry, what can I do to make things right for you?"), you can neutralize it and provide great customer service at the same time.

You can turn angry customers into product evangelists if you treat them correctly. Begin by carefully listening to their problem without interruption. Make sure that they feel they have been heard. After you have heard the problem, thank them for sharing it with you. This is the first step in winning them over. Let them know that they are helping you make your product better. After all, you can't improve on problems you never knew existed. Remember to apologize for the bad experience they had. Customers often aren't looking for justifications; they simply want to know that you are sorry and you are doing the best you can to resolve the issue.

Only after you have apologized should you try to solve their problem. Remember to provide customers with both information and solutions. Ask them what solution they are seeking if it isn't obvious. Be sure to reach an agreement on what the solution will be. It's easy to miscommunicate, so repeat the solution back to them to be sure you are talking about the same thing.

After a solution has been agreed on, solve the problem in an expedient manner. If customers see quick results, they feel valued and will look upon your business favorably. Finally, follow up at a later date to be certain that your solution worked. Your follow-up lets the customer know that you really care about them.

Remember that the customers who take the time to complain are often the most influential. After all, they cared enough about your app to contact you; most customers don't. Even if you lose money on one customer, if they come away with a positive experience, you might benefit from multiple follow-on sales.

Customer Relationship Management

Customer Relationship Management (CRM) refers to software that helps companies manage their sales, marketing, and customer support. In the context of customer support, CRM software can be as simple as a ticket system that helps you track customer issues. Often customer issues will not be solved with a single phone call, so having a way to track the progress of customer issues can become a logistical problem. Nothing is worse for your company's reputation than dropping customer issues before they are solved. CRM software can track issues, beginning with the first e-mail and ending with a complete solution.

There are numerous CRM solutions out there, and we encourage you to Google your way to greater understanding of the space. As a starting point, we can recommend the following two online solutions, both of which are good enough to get you started:

- **insightly.com**: Integrates with Google Apps and Gmail, and provides both CRM and project management. It is free for up to 3 users (customer service reps) and 2,500 contacts.

- **mojohelpdesk.com**: Basic ticket tracking system that enables you to submit tickets by e-mail and includes alerts and reminders. The basic version (with a 30-day free trial) costs $24/month. It supports up to 11 users (customer service reps) with an unlimited number of contacts.

Online Help

Online help can be as simple as basic instructions on how to use your app. You might think the user interface is completely intuitive, but less-savvy users might still want a written description of how to use your app. For many apps, a basic tutorial can be written in a few paragraphs. Time you spend writing basic instructions will save you lots of time helping customers over e-mail. Additionally, many customers will simply uninstall your app if they can't figure out how to use it, which will result in not just lost opportunities but also bad reviews.

After you have help online, it is fairly straightforward to launch a browser from within your app that points at your online help. Doing this gives you in-app help with the benefit that you have to update your help instructions in only one place. You can also consider writing a FAQ on the web site, which should address the most common user questions. Numerous online web site–building apps exist to build your online help site. We have had great results with www.weebly.com.

A lot of applications include a quick tutorial window, with the option for the user to disable the tutorial after the first use. You might consider the option of the tutorial window if your testing group finds that your application is not as intuitive as you thought it was.

E-mail Support

E-mail is perhaps the most common way an app developer interacts with customers. Unless you have a very established app with significant margins, you cannot afford to provide phone support. Be sure and save all your interactions with customers. Often a previous e-mail response can be reused for a new customer with a similar question or problem. Be careful to use good spelling and grammar in e-mail. Nothing says "amateur" like a poorly constructed response. Another aspect of e-mail support that says "amateur" is when you use a mail service such as gmail.com or yahoo.com. If you haven't done so already, take the time to create a custom domain for your e-mail service. Because e-mail is so important, consider providing a way to launch an e-mail app from within your Android application. This is relatively easy to do, as shown here:

```
Intent emailIntent = new Intent(android.content.Intent.ACTION_SEND);
emailIntent.setType("text/plain");
emailIntent.putExtra(Intent.EXTRA_EMAIL, new String[] { "your@email.address" });
startActivity(emailIntent);
```

Forums

Forums can be a great way to help customers help each other, which reduces the workload for the developer. By using a forum, a developer can post help responses that will be read by the entire community of users. Forums can be added to Weebly using the techniques discussed at this site: http://weeblyforums.com/2011/07/how-to-create-a-forum-in-weebly/.

Listening to the Customer

When you first write an app, you have specific ideas about how it will be used. Often your customers will surprise you. By listening to your customers, you can build an app the way they actually want it to be, instead of merely guessing.

You should always prominently list your contact information within your app, so that users have an easy way to get in touch with you if they have comments, concerns, or issues. It is best if you have launched a web site, and that web site also includes a way for customers to reach you. If you can afford the cost and overhead, listing a phone number is great, too. You want all the feedback you can get! You might even consider using an inbound call center. While not cheap, it certainly creates the impression of professionalism. Note that although some inbound call centers charge by the minute, they often have minimum fees, so this option makes sense only if you are expecting to earn quite a bit on a per-customer basis.

Roy has had great feedback from his customers and has learned about use cases for some of his apps that he never even considered. In fact, he even had one user who volunteered to improve the user interface for his BPMDetector app for free! That's quite a payoff just for listening to your users!

Google Play Statistics

Google Play's Android Developer Console is a great resource that Google provides to Android developers. The Developer Console includes statistical information on your app that enables you to learn about your customers.

The statistics section of the Android Developer Console lets you view graphs for active device installs and total device installs, among other things. Active device installs are the installs of your app that people still have on their phones. Total device installs include the installs that were later removed by users. The ratio between active and total installs lets you see how many users are still using your app. If the ratio was (hypothetically) exactly 1.0, it would mean that every app downloaded was still being used. You want this ratio to be as high as possible because that means your app appeals to your target audience. It also shows that your customers actually find your application useful and are using it instead of just trying it once out of curiosity and then removing it.

The statistics section also includes statistics for use by Android version. You can compare your statistics to the published overall device statistics available at `http://developer.android.com/about/dashboards/index.html`.

If your statistics differ significantly from the overall statistics, it might mean that your app has a problem when running on that Android version.

Similarly, statistics on Android devices tell you the most popular hardware platforms (phones and tablets) for your app. You can use this information to prioritize testing of your app; you should try hard to be sure your app has been tested on the most popular platforms.

Finally, statistical information on country and language can let you know where in the world your app is most popular. You can compare the popularity of your app to the average for your application category. This information can be useful to uncover language issues (perhaps you should add human-translated foreign language XML files instead of relying on auto-translate?).

Also, app popularity in certain countries might mean that you should support their language in order to further boost your app's marketability in that region. You can see in Figure 10-1 that one of Roy's apps is being downloaded more often than normal in the United Kingdom, but at below average percentage for its category in South Korea. He would probably improve downloads in that country if he offered a good quality Korean translation.

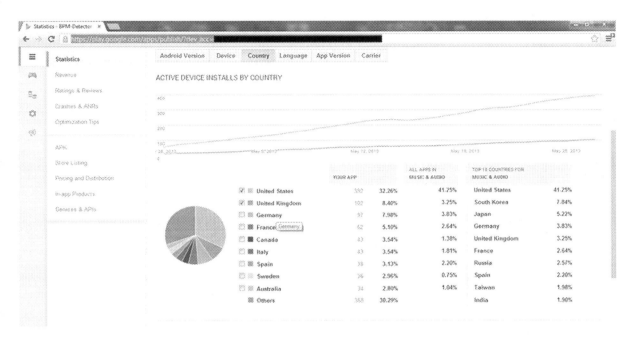

Figure 10-1. Active device installs by country/region for one of Roy's apps

You can use this information to figure out important information about how your application is progressing. For example, you might notice that your application is not being downloaded on certain models of Android phones. Uh-oh! Does that mean that your application is having problems downloading on that particular type of phone? That is most certainly worth looking into.

Perhaps the most useful information the Google Play Developer Console provides is information you never want to see: crash and application not responding (ANR) reports. An ANR typically occurs when your application hogs a resource that prevents the user interface from interacting with the user. This is a serious problem that should be addressed right away. An application crash is exactly what it sounds like, and is also something that should be corrected right away.

The Developer Console not only shows you statistical data on the frequency of each crash or ANR but it also gives you specific information on where the crash or ANR occurred in your source code, which makes it easier to track down and correct. Because the Developer Console keeps track of how many crashes or ANRs of each type have occurred, you can prioritize your bug fixing and go after the most commonly occurring problems first.

Hopefully, you can use this data to discover problems before your users start complaining about them in the form of negative reviews!

Analytics

Although Google Play Statistics gives you some information about your app, if you truly want to see what your users are doing, you need to use Google Analytics. The Google Analytics software development kit (SDK) for Android allows you to easily track key user engagement data, including the number of active application users, usage of specific application features, in-app purchases, and nearly anything else within your application.

Google Analytics supports an "EasyTracker" implementation that allows you to get up and running quickly with basic analytics capabilities for your app. The default EasyTracker example provides you with a way to measure app installations, active users and their demographics, screens and user engagement, as well as crashes and exceptions. Although the Developer Console already tracks system crashes for you, the ability to track exceptions can be a very powerful debugging tool. Simply place code like this in your app:

```
try {
    ...
} catch (IOException e) {
        Tracker myTracker = EasyTracker.getTracker();      // Get a reference to the tracker.
        myTracker.sendException(e.getMessage(), false);    // false ➤ non-fatal exception.
}
```

You can then get a message every time this exception occurs. It is great for tracking how often nonfatal exceptions occur in your code. Often you make assumptions about how frequently (or rarely) exceptions occur, and a better understanding of their frequency can help you improve your application.

You can learn the steps for setting up EasyTracker here:
https://developers.google.com/analytics/devguides/collection/android/v2/#analytics-xml

The Google Analytics SDK can also measure the effectiveness of your mobile marketing campaigns. For example, you could measure how many users were directed to download your app from the Google Play site. Perhaps they clicked that link you have on your web site, clicked an ad you purchased, or maybe they discovered your app from a link within a different app that you have. Either way, you can learn the details using Google Analytics. If you want a way to quantify the success of your marketing campaigns, this is the way to do it. Learn how from the source:
https://developers.google.com/analytics/devguides/collection/android/v2/campaigns

Similarly, you can learn about your user's interactions with social networks. Want to know if they're clicking that Facebook "Like" widget? Want to find out if they're using the Tweet button? Google Analytics can do that as well. The details are here:
https://developers.google.com/analytics/devguides/collection/android/v2/social

Google Analytics is a very powerful, extensible API that includes the potential for custom metrics. Nearly anything you can imagine can be measured. Learn about custom metrics here:
https://developers.google.com/analytics/devguides/collection/android/v2/customdimsmets

You can download the Google Analytics SDK for Android here:
https://developers.google.com/analytics/devguides/collection/android/resources

The API is still in beta, so there might be some rough edges, and things can change at any time.

A/B Testing

All your feedback from users and analytics might inspire you to add a bunch of new features. But how can you be sure which feature is best? A/B testing is the process of scientifically trying two different features to determine which one is favored by your users.

The basic idea behind A/B testing is simple. If you deploy multiple versions of the same app, each version having a difference in a particular feature, and you have a bunch of users who try each of the two features, you can learn which one is better by comparing the results of the two groups of users.

For example, if you have a Click To Buy button on your app, is it better if the button is a standard size, or does a big button generate more click-throughs? You can A/B test to find out. If 1,000 of your users see the standard size button, and 1,000 other users see the big button, you can compare click-through rates to determine which button size will give you better results.

Particularly when it comes to measuring ad campaigns, Google Analytics can be used to do A/B testing. There are, however, other options that are designed from the ground up for A/B testing.

Arise.io (`http://arise.io`) provides developers with an easy way to A/B test their apps. By installing a JAR file in your app and then writing simple test code, you can very easily introduce A/B tests into your apps. See Figure 10-2 for an example. Arise.io is in beta and is currently free for personal and nonprofit apps. When released, the commercial version will probably introduce pricing tiers, although the lowest tiers are likely to be relatively affordable.

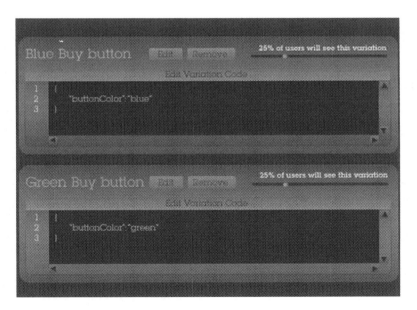

Figure 10-2. An example from the Arise.io web site: `http://arise.io/features/`

Amazon provides A/B testing as a feature, but you need to place the app in its app store. A/B testing with Amazon is free, and might just be the reason you need to finally deploy in its store. You can learn more here: `https://developer.amazon.com/sdk/ab-testing.html`

Figure out the Season of Your Application

We're sure you are quite familiar with Angry Birds because it is very difficult to talk about successful applications without mentioning Rovio's hit mobile game. Rovio decided that Angry Birds was not enough for its fans so it created Angry Birds Seasons in Fall 2010. Angry Birds Seasons has the same rules of the original game, with the slingshot and the attempt to destroy the evil green pigs. The only difference is that the environments are "seasonal." The first version was Trick or Treat, and it was Halloween-themed with pumpkins as well as various other black-and-orange props (see Figure 10-3).

Figure 10-3. Rovio's Angry Birds Seasons is an entirely different application than its very popular Angry Birds predecessor, designed for many seasons

Because the first Angry Birds Seasons was a hit, Rovio followed it up with an update called Seasons Greedings, which used a Christmas holiday theme. In 2011, Rovio improved Seasons with Hogs and Kisses (Valentine's Day–themed), Go Green, Get Lucky (St. Patrick's Day–themed), and Easter Eggs (we probably don't need to tell you its theme). Rovio released a summer-themed Angry Birds Seasons (Summer Pignic), along with more seasons with puns related to birds and pigs. It even released another version of Angry Birds known as Angry Birds Rio. This game is a movie tie-in from *Rio*, a computer animated movie about birds. After another version called Angry Birds Space, Angry Birds is now even embedded in another famous franchise, with the release of Angry Birds Star Wars.

Rovio realized that it needed to let Angry Birds grow and evolve. We agree with its decision not to change the gameplay itself, which is why it created new versions, and gave them new themes, anticipating the changing of seasons. Rovio also planned for the release of *Rio*, and the movie's success helped promote the game.

In the same manner, you can drive more traffic to your app by updating it in ways that reflect the season. Simple things like an updated background or splash screen can renew interest in your app. Nearly every month has a holiday you can leverage to customize your app. Some events, such as holidays, happen on a specific day around the same time of the year. Other events are more ambiguous, based on a mood of the season. Use the seasons to your advantage; anything that grabs a user's interest can help keep your app downloads rolling in.

Plan Around Holidays and Moods

When Mark worked in retail, there were sections of the store that were seasonal and planned for consumers' needs during certain times of the year.

In February, it was Valentine's Day, and the seasonal aisles were decorated with red, pink, and white cards and candy. It then shifted to Easter; the candy was in different packaging with baskets and plastic grass. During summertime, these aisles were filled with squirt guns, portable swimming pools, kites, and other outdoor toys. Then came Back to School time in August and September, and these aisles were filled with pencils, paper, and other school supplies. In October, it was candy again, with spooky Halloween costumes and paraphernalia thrown in. We'll leave you to imagine what was in the aisles in November and December, in anticipation of Christmas.

The reason why we bring up the subject of the seasonal aisle is that it is easy to plan what items will sell at these given times. Holidays are just one event that you can plan around. It is more than just holidays; also the general mood during that time.

In January, people are all about New Years' resolutions and bettering themselves, which is a good time to sell health and productivity applications. Because Valentine's Day is in February, people tend to think of love and relationships, so it is a good time to market an application related to that mood. Any application related to vacation planning probably sells well during spring and summer periods. By now, you can see a pattern forming, and we'll let you guess what kind of applications sell around Christmas time.

Because you figured out the purpose of your application in Chapter 2, you should be able to figure out during what times of the year it will sell the most. It might be a certain holiday or just some time of the year when people will be thinking about doing a certain thing that your application can help them with. Plan for this time and get the word out to your contacts at this time.

Figure Out Your "Peak Period," if Any

After your app is in the marketplace, you might discover that it has a "peak period" during which it sells exceptionally well for whatever reasons, but has few downloads outside of this time period.

For example, if you create an application that follows NCAA college basketball games, you will see an increase during the "March Madness" tournament, but then nothing until the next basketball season. Perhaps your application will have a longer peak period. For a tax preparation application, for example, you will see a lot of downloads during the months of January to April as people prepare for the April 15th U.S. income tax deadline but only a few downloads by procrastinators in May. Your application could be completely forgotten during summer or fall.

If one of your applications has a peak period, you might have trouble making money year-round. A better strategy is to have many applications going at once and to focus on each app during its peak season. You can use the nonpeak off-season to prepare for updates for next year (or simply write an app that is less peaky). Also, remember that the holiday season is almost always the busiest time of year, and the first few months after the holidays can be slow. These sorts of annual fluctuations are common in many markets.

The Price

By now, your application is out on the market and has a price, even if it is free. You might be using that suggestion in Chapter 6 about having a paid version and a free version.

Although Google Play does not let you change an unpaid app into a paid app, you can always change the pricing of your paid apps.

Because the price can be changed, you might want to experiment with your application's price, just to see how your users react. One developer told us that he had a $.99 application, and he upped the price from $.99 to $1.99 for a week, then to $2.99, and then to $3.99. What he learned was that he had 100 sales in a week at $.99; then he had about 45 sales at $1.99. He made less over all... but close. Then he upped the price of the application to $2.99, and he still had 45 sales—roughly 136 percent of the $.99 app revenue. That's not bad.

The Economics of App Pricing

In some cases, then, you can raise the price of your app and make more money. In other cases, raising the price will cause you to make less money than you potentially would have. Economists talk about the "price elasticity of demand." The idea is that for some purchases, people will be very sensitive to pricing. The demand will decrease quickly as the price goes up. For example, if your favorite soft drink is suddenly more expensive than all the others, you'd probably switch to a different drink. On the other hand, some purchases are very "inelastic." People just *have* to make these purchases, regardless of price. The cost of taking your child to the pediatrician is a good example of this. You're going to pay for it, even if the price goes up.

So is your app more like a soft drink or more like a visit to the pediatrician? Well, this is a lot like the vitamin versus pain-killer comparison we discussed in Chapter 2. If your app is a pain-killer, it's going to get something closer to pediatrician pricing. On the other hand, vitamins often get priced like soda. You can see that the price customers are willing to pay often depends on the *necessity* of the app.

There are other factors as well. If you're the only game in town, you can charge more. So if you're the only solution to a problem, users will have to buy your app to solve the problem. On the other hand, if there are lots of other equivalent solutions, at some point there will be a "race to the bottom." That means that all the players offering solutions will have to compete with each other on price, which will drive the price down for everyone over time. We can call this factor the *availability of equivalent solutions*.

The characteristics of your user base are other factors that determine price. If you're selling to law firms, you can ask for a higher price than if you sell to teenagers. Obviously, *who's paying for it* is a factor.

Finally, *branding* is a factor. If you know that an app is made by Oracle, Microsoft, or any other big player, you expect a certain minimum level of quality. These companies are well-known brands, and people will always pay more for the well-known brand. Be sure to create and foster your brand identity as you bring new apps to market.

When to Price High

No consumer likes a price increase. But the fact is, a price increase can be very good for you. Price increases happen all the time in the business world, and you should not hesitate to increase your product's price if it makes you more money. Naturally, if your app is necessary (it's a pain-killer) with no equivalent solutions, and you have customers with deep pockets and a great brand, you should start with a high price. You can always lower your price and see how that affects your price elasticity of demand curve.

You can even play around with increasing the price of your app during peak periods or your app's "season." Perhaps your app has a lower elasticity-of-demand in its peak season. If so, you'll make more money overall with a higher price.

When to Price Low

On the other hand if your app isn't really necessary (it's a vitamin) with lots of equivalent solutions, your customers have limited means, and your brand isn't well known, you should start with a low price. You can always increase your price and see how that affects your price elasticity of demand curve.

Occasionally, you will discover that your application isn't working out the way you expected it to. You might discover that there have been very few downloads.

Besides trying new marketing routes to inform more people about your application, you can try to increase sales by marking the app down. You can even consider making it an ad-supported app and give it away for free. That's better than not making any sales at all. If the application is just totally hopeless, it might be worth taking it off the market entirely just so it doesn't diminish your brand simply by being associated with you.

You might have a simple problem child that just needs to be improved before the real sales on it begin. If so, we recommend a temporary price decrease on the current version. You have to get the word out through your media outlets, social networks, and other methods of informing your target market that you are doing this.

We have discovered that news of a price reduction can often lead to rumors about the demise of a product. For example, when Nintendo reduced the price of the GameCube to $99.99, it looked pretty bad for the company. As it turns out, it was a way to compete with Sony and Microsoft until the Wii could be launched. In other words, if you spread the word about a price reduction on your application, don't be surprised if someone else spreads the word saying that your application is dying. But hey, there's no such thing as bad press, right? This is the perfect time to prove them wrong by releasing an updated version.

This way, Android users discover something worthwhile at a lower price. Then, by the time the application goes back to the regular price, people are more willing to pay it because the app has been improved.

Keep Moving Forward

We have essentially finished discussing marketing your Android Application. Let us give you one last bit of advice: Keep moving forward when it comes to your applications. If you want to start a career as an Android developer, you have to continually create new applications as well as improve on the older ones. That can be a difficult juggling act.

The important thing is that you keep on trying, keep on learning, and keep advancing your career. This is a time when you want to hold on to milestones such as your one millionth download or one thousandth download. You keep those milestones around not so you can brag but so you can keep track of your progress.

We have found that programming applications is rewarding because there is a certain joy that comes from creating something new. Although this book is intended to teach you to be a successful app developer, financial success is easiest to attain when your heart is in your work. Create something that you are truly proud of and you will profit, both financially and personally.

We wish you the best in bringing your app ideas to life and hope that you find the journey as rewarding as the destination.

Summary

- Do your users have an easy way to get in touch with you? Preferably more than one way?

- Are you tracking customer support issues and reducing your support workload?

- Do you monitor Google statistics for trends and modify your app accordingly?

- Have you integrated analytics into your app to improve your understanding of customer motivations?

- Do you use A/B testing to improve your app?

- Do you need to change your app after its release?

- Is there a "peak season" for your app?

- Do you need to do a price increase/decrease?

And the last and most important question: Are you moving forward?

Index